SIDREA Series in Accounting and Business Administration

Mauro Paoloni, University of Roma Tor Vergata
Roma, Italy

Paola Paoloni, University of Roma Sapienza
Roma, Italy

Patrizia Pastore, University of Calabria
Rende, Italy

Angela Kate Pettinicchio, Catholic University of the Sacred Heart
Milano, Italy

Mauro Romano, University of Bari Aldo Moro
Bari, Italy

Pasquale Ruggiero, University of Siena
Siena, Italy

Marcantonio Ruisi, University of Palermo
Palermo, Italy

Claudio Teodori, University of Brescia
Brescia, Italy

Simone Terzani, University of Perugia
Perugia, Italy

Stefania Veltri, University of Calabria
Rende, Italy

This is the official book series of SIDREA - the Italian Society of Accounting and Business Administration. This book series is provided with a wide Scientific Committee composed of Academics by SIDREA. It publishes contributions (monographs, edited volumes and proceedings) as a result of the double blind review process by the SIDREA's thematic research groups, operating at the national and international levels. Particularly, the series aims to disseminate specialized findings on several topics – classical and cutting-edge alike – that are currently being discussed by the accounting and business administration communities. The series authors are respected researchers and professors in the fields of business valuation; governance and internal control; financial accounting; public accounting; management control; gender; turnaround predictive models; non-financial disclosure; intellectual capital, smart technologies, and digitalization; and university governance and performance measurement.This book series is indexed in Scopus.

Ilaria Mastrorocco

From Voluntary Responsibility to Regulatory Compliance

Analysing Corporate Responses to the Human Rights Due Diligence Framework in the EU

Springer

Ilaria Mastrorocco
Casamassima (70010)
LUM Giuseppe Degennaro University
Puglia, Italy

ISSN 2662-9879 ISSN 2662-9887 (electronic)
SIDREA Series in Accounting and Business Administration
ISBN 978-3-032-34491-5 ISBN 978-3-032-34492-2 (eBook)
https://doi.org/10.1007/978-3-032-34492-2

This Springer imprint is published by the registered company Springer Nature Switzerland AG
The registered company address is: Gewerbestrasse 11, 6330 Cham, Switzerland

To my family, for their unconditional love, constant support, and unwavering belief in me throughout this journey.

Preface

In recent years, the issue of business and human rights has taken on increasing prominence in academic, institutional, and managerial debates on corporate responsibility, sustainability, and global governance. Businesses are no longer assessed solely based on their ability to generate economic value, but also in relation to their capacity to identify, prevent, mitigate, and report on the negative impacts that their direct or indirect activities may have on individuals, communities, and society.

In this context, human rights due diligence has progressively established itself as one of the main tools through which corporate human rights responsibility can be translated into concrete practices. Since the adoption of the United Nations Guiding Principles on Business and Human Rights, human rights due diligence has become a fundamental benchmark for businesses, institutions, and academics. However, despite the growing attention paid to this issue, its implementation remains uneven. Many companies continue to approach this practice primarily as a formal or communicative compliance exercise, whilst its substantive integration into governance processes, corporate strategies, and decision-making mechanisms remains a significant challenge.

This monograph addresses these issues in a timely and highly topical manner. The work examines human rights due diligence from both a conceptual and an empirical perspective, paying particular attention to the regulatory changes introduced by the Corporate Sustainability Due Diligence Directive. The CSDDD represents a significant turning point in the European and international landscape, as it helps shift human rights due diligence from a predominantly voluntary framework towards a more binding and institutionalised one. This transition raises crucial questions about how companies respond to regulatory pressures, manage stakeholder expectations, and pursue their social legitimacy.

One of the monograph's main strengths lies in its ability to integrate different levels of analysis. Firstly, the monograph reviews the state of the art in the literature through a systematic literature review, identifying the main strands of research, areas that remain fragmented, and possible future trajectories. Subsequently, the work develops a conceptual framework grounded in institutional theory, highlighting the role of coercive, regulatory, and mimetic pressures in shaping corporate behaviour in the face of new due diligence obligations.

Finally, the book offers an empirical analysis of companies' preparedness for the CSDDD, integrating institutional theory and legitimacy theory to understand the factors driving the adoption of human rights due diligence.

This integrated perspective permits moving beyond a purely regulatory interpretation of the phenomenon. Regulation is not viewed merely as a set of legal obligations but as part of a broader process through which companies seek to maintain their legitimacy, respond to pressures from the institutional environment, and adapt to an evolving social context. In this sense, the volume contributes to a more nuanced understanding of the opportunities and limitations of mandatory human rights due diligence. On the one hand, regulation can foster greater convergence towards shared standards and incentivise companies to strengthen their practices. On the other hand, there remains a risk that such practices will be adopted in a predominantly symbolic manner or with a focus on mere compliance, without genuine integration into organisational processes.

The empirical analysis presented in this volume further enriches this debate. By examining a global sample of companies and assessing changes in human rights due diligence practices considering the introduction of the CSDDD, the study provides initial evidence of the Directive's anticipatory effect. This is a particularly significant contribution, as much of the debate on mandatory human rights due diligence has so far been predominantly theoretical, legal, or regulatory in nature. The findings, however, provide useful insights for scholars, policymakers, and practitioners interested in understanding how regulatory change might influence corporate behaviour and which conditions favour the adoption of more structured human rights protection practices.

The monograph also makes a significant contribution by addressing one of the key challenges in the field of business and human rights: bridging the gap between principles and practice. International standards have played a fundamental role in defining corporate responsibilities, but their effectiveness depends on the ability to translate them into governance systems, managerial routines, and accountability mechanisms. By focusing on the evolution, determinants, and implications of human rights due diligence, the volume helps to advance the debate on how companies can move from making formal commitments to a more concrete implementation of human rights responsibilities.

This monograph therefore represents a rigorous and timely contribution to the literature on business and human rights, corporate sustainability, and responsible business conduct. It offers valuable insights not only for the academic community but also for policymakers and professionals called upon to address the new challenges posed by sustainability regulation and the growing demand for accountability along global value chains.

Puglia, Italy Ilaria Mastrorocco

Competing Interests The author has no competing interests to declare that are relevant to the content of this manuscript.

Contents

About the Author

Ilaria Mastrorocco is a PhD at LUM "Giuseppe Degennaro" University, Department of Management, Finance and Technology, Casamassima (Bari). Her main research interests are in the fields of accounting and business administration, particularly in relation to CSR, ESG rating, and social behaviour.

List of Abbreviations

ATT	Average Treatment Effect on the Treated
BHR	Business and Human Rights
CCMC	China's Due Diligence Guidance for Responsible Mineral Supply Chains
CHRB	Corporate Human Rights Benchmark
CSR	Corporate Social Responsibility
CSRD	Corporate Sustainability Reporting Directive
CSDDD	Corporate Sustainability Due Diligence Directive
DiD	Difference-in-Differences
EBSCO	Elton B. Stephens Company (database)
ERM	Enterprise Risk Management
ESG	Environmental, Social and Governance
ESRS	European Sustainability Reporting Standards
GRI	Global Reporting Initiative
HRIA	Human Rights Impact Assessment
HRDD	Human Rights Due Diligence
HREDD	Human Rights and Environmental Due Diligence
ILO	International Labour Organization
IB	International Business
ISSB	International Sustainability Standards Board
LSEG	London Stock Exchange Group
mHRDD	Mandatory Human Rights Due Diligence
MNC	Multinational Corporation
NFRD	Non-Financial Reporting Directive
NGO	Non-Governmental Organisation
OECD	Organisation for Economic Co-operation and Development
OHCHR	Office of the United Nations High Commissioner for Human Rights
PRISMA	Preferred Reporting Items for Systematic Reviews and Meta-Analyses
RAFI	Reporting and Assurance Frameworks Initiative
ROA	Return on Assets
SCDD	Supply Chain Due Diligence
SDGs	Sustainable Development Goals

SLR	Systematic Literature Review
SME	Small and Medium-sized Enterprise
UN	United Nations
UNGPs	United Nations Guiding Principles on Business and Human Rights
VIF	Variance Inflation Factor
WBA	World Benchmarking Alliance

List of Figures

List of Tables

Chapter 1
Introduction

1.1 Historical Development

The issue of business and human rights falls within the broader scope of the so-called grand challenges, that is, those major global challenges that have a significant impact on various actors worldwide, with particular reference to multinational corporations (MNCs) in the field of international business (IB) studies. These challenges mainly concern environmental degradation, migration, poverty, and inequality. Within this framework, the social dimension also includes human rights, defined as "fundamental rights to which every individual is inherently entitled as a human being" (Wettstein et al., 2019). Since these rights are universal in nature, their protection concerns all actors, including businesses and managers (Olsen et al., 2025).

The historical development of human rights in the corporate sphere dates back to the period following the Second World War, in particular to the founding of the International Labour Organisation (ILO) in 1919 and the recognition of international labour standards in 1944 (ILO, 2025). The ILO, as a specialised agency of the United Nations (UN), was established to regulate and protect human rights in the business context, promoting decent working conditions, safety, and respect for human dignity globally.

Over time, numerous international initiatives have sought to strengthen corporate responsibility in the field of human rights, culminating in the "Protect, Respect and Remedy" framework proposed by Ruggie in 2008. This approach laid the foundations for the development of the United Nations Guiding Principles on Business and Human Rights (UNGPs), which were officially adopted in 2011 (Hubers & Thijssens, 2023). These developments, together with the growing interest shown by national institutions and the private sector, have contributed to the emergence of an interdisciplinary field of study known as Business and Human Rights (BHR). According to Ramasastry (2015), BHR is a discipline that "guides businesses, states

I. Mastrorocco, *From Voluntary Responsibility to Regulatory Compliance*, SIDREA Series in Accounting and Business Administration,
https://doi.org/10.1007/978-3-032-34492-2_1

and societies towards assessing corporate conduct in light of the universal principles of human rights enshrined in major international treaties". Similarly, Schrempf-Stirling and Van Buren (2020) describe BHR as a field of study aimed at analysing the responsibility of companies for human rights violations committed directly or through their subsidiaries, as well as the various forms of complicity that can arise along global value chains (Bernaz, 2016).

In the 1980s, a series of serious human rights violations by multinational companies, particularly in the textile and technology sectors, led public debate on the issue of Business and Human Rights (BHR) (Morán-Muñoz et al., 2024). These incidents, which were particularly prevalent in areas characterised by poverty and conflict, such as Sierra Leone, attracted the attention of non-governmental organisations (NGOs) and public opinion, prompting international institutions to develop regulatory frameworks aimed at strengthening corporate accountability. It is in this context that the UN Global Compact was created in 2000, representing a concrete response to the growing global interest in the issue of BHR. The initiative remains one of the most comprehensive frameworks on corporate responsibility, as it aims to align business practices with key international human rights standards, including the Universal Declaration of Human Rights, the fundamental ILO Conventions, the Rio Declaration on Environment and Development, and the United Nations Convention against Corruption (UNGC, 2020). The Global Compact marked a paradigm shift in the concept of corporate responsibility, moving beyond a purely economic vision to include social and environmental dimensions of corporate governance.

Its principles are divided into four fundamental areas: human rights, labour, the environment, and anti-corruption, thus helping to bridge the gap between BHR and Corporate Social Responsibility (CSR) (Podrecca et al., 2022).

A further crucial step in the evolution of the human rights debate was the adoption of the United Nations Guiding Principles on Business and Human Rights (UNGPs), developed over 6 years by Professor John Ruggie, as Special Representative of the United Nations Secretary-General. Unlike previous initiatives, the UNGPs placed greater emphasis on the duty of states to protect human rights, while introducing specific responsibilities for businesses based on the "protect, respect and remedy" paradigm. In particular, Pillar II of the UNGPs is the central reference point for the literature on BHR, as it defines the "responsibility" of companies to respect human rights, as distinct from a legal obligation in the strict sense (Deva & Bilchitz, 2013). This responsibility implies not only a negative duty not to cause harm, but also the adoption of human rights policies, the performance of ongoing due diligence activities, and the implementation of mechanisms to prevent and remedy negative impacts (Al-Shaer et al., 2024; Schrempf-Stirling et al., 2022; Ruggie, 2013).

As Muchlinski (2012) observes, these developments can be considered "significant, if not revolutionary" for the evolution of corporate responsibility and governance.

Ruggie's work has also promoted a "polycentric" approach, shifting the focus from an exclusively state-centric conception of responsibility to a global model involving both public and private actors. However, this approach has not been without criticism, particularly for the risk of an imbalance between the responsibilities assigned to states and those assigned to businesses (Wettstein, 2013). McConnell (2016) provocatively argues that while states have progressively failed to guarantee the protection of human rights, the influence of businesses has grown. Furthermore, the non-binding nature of the UNGPs has been the subject of further criticism, as although they outline corporate responsibilities, they do not provide for coercive enforcement mechanisms (Oliveira & Silveira, 2023).

In recent years, the United Nations has adopted Agenda 2030, which is divided into 17 Sustainable Development Goals (SDGs). These goals represent a significant step forward as they are consistent with the UNGPs and recognise the central role of businesses as global partners in promoting environmental sustainability and protecting human rights, which are essential for the well-being of individuals. The founding principle of the Agenda, summarised in the expression "leaving no one behind", clearly reflects this inclusive vision of sustainable development (Winkler & Williams, 2017). Although the 2030 Agenda places a strong emphasis on climate change and environmental sustainability, several goals, in particular SDGs 3, 5, 6, 8, 16, and 17, directly or indirectly address the issue of human rights. These goals are closely linked to ILO conventions and are rooted in the fundamental principles of the United Nations, which are oriented not only towards "doing no harm" but also towards actively promoting human well-being and development ("doing good") (Buhmann, 2024). There is also a strong conceptual link between the SDGs and the UNGPs: the latter provide a framework for the implementation of the 2030 Agenda goals, emphasising human freedom and the ability to pursue sustainable development, as well as the need to review the criteria used to assess the rights of those involved. In this perspective, companies are called upon to reorient their activities to reduce the risks associated with business operations and to contribute, through goods and services, to the achievement of sustainable development goals (Buhmann, 2024).

Since their adoption, the SDGs have taken on a strategic role for businesses, profoundly influencing their choices and behaviour. They represent both a framework for promoting sustainability and a fundamental tool for achieving moral and operational legitimacy (Buhmann et al., 2019). Adherence to the SDGs allows companies to demonstrate their commitment to widely recognised principles such as environmental protection, respect for human rights, and social justice (Zagelmeyer & Sinkovics, 2019). This, in turn, helps to strengthen corporate reputation, facilitate access to sustainable financing, and increase stakeholder confidence.

Despite the progress made in the field of BHR and the growing attention from national and international institutions, numerous unresolved issues remain in the academic debate, especially in relation to the persistence of human rights violations by companies. The literature continues to grapple with definitional problems, the identification of the boundaries of research, and the distinction between direct and indirect impacts of corporate activities (Oliveira & Silveira, 2023). Furthermore, the COVID-19 pandemic has further exacerbated the difficulties in ensuring fair working conditions and regulating global value chains, highlighting the urgency of strengthening corporate practices on human rights (Voss, 2020).

1.2 Literature Review

This section examines the main perspectives that have been adopted over time to analyse the field of BHR research. The literature on BHR mainly questions the existence of human rights obligations on companies and the concrete meaning of these obligations for business activities (Schrempf-Stirling & Van Buren III, 2024). The evolution of the concept of human rights and its implications for corporate governance, responsibility, and sustainability highlight the need for an increasingly interdisciplinary approach. Today, BHR research is being conducted in a variety of fields, including international policy, national regulation, corporate governance, and management studies (Wettstein, 2021). Within the latter field, four main areas of analysis have emerged: workers' rights, consumer protection, impact on local communities, and environmental responsibility (Zagelmeyer, 2020). Concerning the latter dimension, one of the most debated issues concerns the relationship between BHR and CSR (Ullah et al., 2021).

The theoretical basis for the link between BHR and CSR has its roots in the origins of the literature on corporate social responsibility and in the ethical perspective of corporate responsibility (Carroll, 1999). Dempsey (1949), in his pioneering work *Roots of Business Responsibility*, argued that businesses should contribute to the well-being of society. Similarly, Heald (1988) and Bowen (1953) emphasised the ethical dimension of entrepreneurial activity, becoming some of the first authors to anticipate the principles underlying BHR (Ramasastry, 2015).

More recently, the integration of corporate responsibility for human rights into CSR has been reinforced through the concept of human rights due diligence promoted by the UNGPs. In line with these principles, companies are called upon to adopt a "know and show" approach, typical of CSR, which implies the ability to identify, prevent, and report on human rights impacts. Furthermore, the growing use of performance indicators and measurement tools to assess respect for human rights is closely linked to CSR and non-financial reporting practices (Favotto & Kollman, 2022). These developments are particularly relevant considering growing social expectations and pressures from formal and informal institutions, which companies are called upon to manage.

The European approach to CSR reinforces this stance by explicitly including HRDD within the corporate social responsibility frameworks (European Commission, 2011). According to this perspective, companies should ensure that their CSR policies are consistent with international social and human rights standards, such as the OECD Guidelines for Multinational Enterprises, the ISO 26000 standard on social responsibility, and the UNGPs (Ramasastry, 2015). From an academic point of view, some scholars also argue that human rights are intrinsically embedded in the social dimension of ESG criteria, making CSR and BHR complementary concepts (Escrig-Olmedo et al., 2019). Consistently, the sustainability model proposed by Carroll (1999) explicitly integrates ethical dimensions into corporate responsibility, further reinforcing the idea of convergence between the two approaches.

However, the relationship between CSR and BHR remains a subject of debate. Although BHR has often been incorporated into the literature on CSR, human rights have historically occupied a marginal position in its conceptualisation (Welford, 2002). Furthermore, despite the obvious overlaps, the direct application of CSR logic to BHR is a recurring mistake, given the substantial differences between the two concepts (Schrempf-Stirling et al., 2022).

Unlike the lengthy debate on CSR, which emerged in the 1950s and 1960s, the process of institutionalising BHR has mainly developed since the 2000s, thanks to initiatives promoted by the United Nations (Wettstein, 2012). While CSR is traditionally oriented towards promoting positive social impacts, BHR focuses primarily on preventing harm. Furthermore, CSR has often been interpreted as a set of voluntary practices that go "beyond the law", while human rights obligations are generally considered legally binding. CSR has also been conceived as an apolitical field, based on corporate self-regulation, while human rights are intrinsically linked to both national and international political and institutional frameworks (Wettstein, 2020). Finally, while CSR tends to adopt a business-centred perspective, BHR focuses more on the rights and interests of those potentially affected by business activities (Schrempf-Stirling et al., 2022).

One of the perspectives through which literature analyses BHR concerns its integration into management and organisational studies. In this context, two main interpretative approaches can be distinguished. The first conceives BHR as a form of global governance, while the second analyses it through the lens of sensemaking. The Global Governance approach focuses on how state and non-state actors define rules and manage relationships in inter-organisational contexts related to human rights. This perspective emphasises the integration of human rights into corporate practices, analysing the role played by regulatory frameworks, international agreements, and voluntary initiatives in changing corporate behaviour. In this view, governments, multinationals, non-governmental organisations, and supranational institutions interact within a complex system that progressively redefines forms of corporate responsibility in the global economy. The sensemaking approach, on the other hand, focuses on how companies interpret and respond to external stimuli, particularly human rights violations.

This perspective does not view human rights obligations as simply imposed by external governance systems, but analyses how organisations understand, process, and address these issues based on the institutional and social context in which they operate (Schrempf-Stirling & Van Buren III, 2024). It highlights the cognitive and organisational processes through which companies give meaning to human rights issues and integrate them into their decision-making strategies. Taken together, both approaches help to clarify how BHR can be incorporated into different levels of the organisation, considering macro, meso, and micro dimensions of analysis.

Based on these theoretical assumptions, Olsen et al. (2025) propose a "relational" approach to BHR, emphasising that companies must clearly define their responsibilities towards rights-holders, including key stakeholders such as local communities, workers, consumers, and suppliers. This perspective is in line with stakeholder theory, as it highlights the importance for companies to develop solid and lasting relationships with those involved in their activities (Freeman, 1984).

However, in the context of BHR, a central dilemma arises in relation to the value creation process. On the one hand, some scholars argue that respect for human rights can generate value for the company, strengthening its reputation, increasing stakeholder confidence, and promoting long-term sustainability; on the other hand, it is highlighted that the violation of these rights can lead to the destruction of value, with negative consequences in terms of reputation, legal and social issues (Avant et al., 2023).

A significant contribution to the analysis of BHR also comes from the literature on Social Issues in Management (SIM) (Schrempf-Stirling & Van Buren, 2020), which offers a more focused perspective within management studies. This strand focuses on how companies integrate social and ethical dimensions into their organisational structures and practices, conceiving companies not only as economic entities but also as social and political actors. Within this field, BHR has gradually emerged as a sub-strand of research aimed at investigating the reasons why companies have responsibilities in human rights. The literature has analysed corporate responses through tools such as codes of conduct, due diligence frameworks, stakeholder management mechanisms, and soft law instruments, including the UNGC and multi-stakeholder initiatives (Fasterling, 2017; Rice, 2002; Blanton & Blanton, 2006). Despite this, a relatively limited number of studies have systematically examined the concrete effects of corporate human rights initiatives in terms of economic performance, ethical behaviour, and organisational legitimacy.

As already highlighted, BHR is by its nature an interdisciplinary field: originating in legal studies, it has gradually expanded to business ethics, accounting, management, and international business, with a growing focus on corporate responsibility, internal organisational responses, and the relationship between CSR and BHR (Wettstein et al., 2019; Wettstein, 2020). The international roots of human rights regulations, including the Global Compact, the UNGPs, and the International Bill of Human Rights, link BHR and international business studies particularly closely.

In the early stages, these instruments mainly attributed responsibility for preventing human rights violations by companies to States. However, the evolution of global markets and globalisation processes have gradually recognised that companies also have a direct role to play in protecting human rights and providing remedies in the event of violations, especially when these occur along transnational value chains. Nevertheless, it remains difficult to define the nature of corporate responsibilities in a global context. One of the central issues concerns the type of impact exerted by companies: they do not always violate human rights directly, but may be indirectly involved through relationships with suppliers, business partners, or subsidiaries, giving rise to forms of complicity that are difficult to define in legal and operational terms. Two contrasting approaches are commonly used to define corporate responsibility in the field of human rights. The first distinguishes between direct and indirect impacts of corporate activities (Wettstein, 2010), while the second is based on the concept of sphere of influence, which interprets stakeholders as being located within concentric circles of influence exerted by the company (Gasser, 2007). The latter approach has been criticised because it is difficult to determine precisely which entities are involved or responsible in cases of human rights violations. An alternative to this approach is offered by the United Nations Guiding Principles, which establish that companies can be directly responsible for, contribute to, or otherwise be involved in human rights violations (Zagelmeyer, 2020).

Since human rights research is interdisciplinary in nature and uses multiple analytical approaches, the field of BHR remains fragmented, despite the wealth of scientific literature available. Theories such as stakeholder theory, CSR, international business, and social issues in management have contributed significantly to the development of the field, each offering different conceptual and methodological perspectives. However, this heterogeneity makes it difficult to develop a unified and systematic interpretative framework for assessing corporate responsibilities in the field of human rights.

Nevertheless, the protection of human rights is increasingly recognised as an autonomous responsibility of the company, and no longer just an ancillary component of CSR policies, also in light of the evolution of national and international regulatory frameworks. This transformation is set to bring greater consistency and solidity to the field of research, while strengthening the role of corporate responsibility as a central element of ethical governance and sustainable business practices.

1.3 Structure and Aim of the Dissertation

The context described is characterised by growing attention to the field of BHR research, with a specific focus on HRDD and its regulatory evolution. Despite growing interest and extensive scientific production developed over time, articulated according to different disciplinary perspectives, there is still no fully systematised body of studies on the subject. In particular, the literature dedicated to HRDD focuses mainly on three main areas: legal, organisational, and managerial. Although this plurality of approaches allows for a comprehensive reading of the phenomenon, it has not yet allowed for the development of a unified and consolidated theoretical framework.

In light of this scenario, the general objective of the dissertation is to offer a comprehensive contribution to the topic of HRDD from a managerial and accounting perspective. In particular, it aims, on the one hand, to systematically reconstruct the state of the art of the literature on the subject and, on the other, to provide a theoretical and empirical contribution in relation to recent regulatory developments introduced by the Corporate Sustainability Due Diligence Directive (CSDDD).

To achieve this overall objective, the work is divided into three chapters, each of which answers a specific research question and contributes, through different methodological approaches, to the achievement of the overall result.

Chapter 2, entitled "Mapping the Field: A Systematic Literature Review on Human Rights Due Diligence in an Evolving Regulatory Context", stems from the need to clearly outline the state of research on HRDD in the fields of management, accounting, economics, finance, and econometrics. The main research questions addressed are: "What is the current state of the debate on HRDD in management and accounting? What are the main research gaps and avenues for future research?" To this end, a Systematic Literature Review (SLR) was conducted on a sample of 89 articles extracted from the Scopus and EBSCO databases. The analysis provides an overview of the existing literature, highlighting its main characteristics, such as its evolution over time, its distribution by journal and geographical area, and the methodologies adopted. Through content analysis, the contributions were also grouped into five thematic clusters, which allow us to identify the main lines of research and the growing attention paid to regulatory developments in the field. Finally, the chapter highlights the main gaps in the literature and directions for future research.

Chapter 3, entitled "Explaining Corporate Behaviour in the Transition to Mandatory Due Diligence: An Institutional Theory Approach", addresses one of the issues raised by the SLR, namely: "How has HRDD evolved, and what is the institutional impact of the CSDDD on companies' practices?" Through theoretical and conceptual analysis, the chapter examines the fundamental elements of HRDD, its integration into corporate practices, and its institutional and regulatory evolution. Based on this analysis, a theoretical framework is developed to identify the changes expected following the introduction of the CSDDD, considering the institutional pressures exerted on companies. The proposed model highlights the advantages, critical issues, and possible ways of implementing the legislation, helping to reduce the risk of symbolic compliance behaviour.

Chapter 4, "Examining Corporate Readiness for the CSDDD: An Empirical Test of Institutional and Legitimacy Pressures", aims to empirically test the framework developed in the previous chapter, integrating it with legitimacy theory. The related research question is: "How does the adoption of CSDDD affect the adoption of HRDD practices, and how do companies reconcile institutional compliance and legitimacy concerns?"

The empirical analysis, conducted on a global sample of companies belonging to the S&P Global 1200 index, assesses the level of preparedness of European companies, the main targets of the directive, and those operating in countries already characterised by binding due diligence obligations. Institutional and legitimacy factors are also analysed as potential determinants of HRDD performance. Using difference-in-differences analysis, event studies, and longitudinal regressions, the study shows that companies operating in more stringent institutional contexts, which are more internationalised and perform better in the field of human rights, achieve more advanced results in terms of HRDD, in line with institutional theory predictions. Consistent with legitimacy theory, it also emerges that companies that are more exposed to media scrutiny or have a history of human rights violations tend to strengthen their due diligence practices.

Table 1.1 Table of contents

Chapter	Title	RQ	Methodology	Main Results
2.	Mapping the Field: A Systematic Literature Review on Human Rights Due Diligence in an Evolving Regulatory Context	What is the current state of the debate on HRDD in management and accounting? What are the main research gaps and avenues for future research?	Systematic literature review	Definition of five clusters of analysis concerning HRDD topic under an economic and management perspective, and conceptualisation of research gap and future research avenues.
3.	Explaining Corporate Behaviour in the Transition to Mandatory Due Diligence: An Institutional Theory Approach	How has HRDD evolved, and what is the institutional impact of the CSDDD on companies' practices?	Theoretical and conceptual analysis	Theoretical framework analysing the potential impact of CSDDD on HRDD practices on companies according to the institutional theory and definition of potential advantages and disadvantages.
4.	Examining Corporate Readiness for the CSDDD: An Empirical Test of Institutional and Legitimacy Pressures.	How does the adoption of CSDDD affect the adoption of HRDD practices, and how do companies reconcile institutional compliance and legitimacy concerns?	Quantitative research (Dif-in-Dif), event study, panel regression analysis.	The results show that companies respond to emerging regulatory interventions differently according to the institutional background, and that both institutional and legitimacy pressures influence the HRDD practices.

Overall, the monograph contributes to clarifying and deepening the topic of HRDD, offering a significant theoretical and empirical contribution in an area of growing academic, institutional, and operational interest. The overall structure and main objectives of the work are summarised in Table 1.1.

Chapter 2
Mapping the Field: A Systematic Literature Review on Human Rights Due Diligence in an Evolving Regulatory Context

2.1 Introduction

In recent years, the interface between business activities and human rights has become a particularly important topic in the academic and political debate (Arnold, 2016). BHR stream of research has evolved as corporations, especially at the international level, recognise their political and social responsibilities as well as their economic responsibilities (Amengual et al., 2023; Arnold, 2010; Avery, 2021; Ruggie, 2007). As a result, contributions on this topic have analysed the mostly voluntary initiatives taken by companies to mitigate the risks of human rights abuses and reduce their damage, in line with the principles of corporate responsibility (Deva & Bilchitz, 2013; O'Brien & Dhanarajan, 2016). In this respect, the introduction of the UNGPs in 2011 represented a break with the past, as they defined institutional and regulatory guidelines in relation to state and corporate responsibility in this area (Neglia, 2016; Triefus, 2023). The second pillar represents the core of corporate responsibility to respect human rights through the concept of HRDD, which requires companies to recognise, prevent, and mitigate adverse impacts on human rights through their operations and supply chains (Dehbi & Martin-Ortega, 2023; McCorquodale et al., 2017; McCorquodale & Nolan, 2021). The literature on HRDD is divided into different perspectives. Legal research has examined the regulatory purpose and the evolution between voluntary and mandatory regulations, while organisational research has observed implementation in companies, especially in multinational corporations and supply chains (Bonnitcha & McCorquodale, 2017; Schrempf-Stirling & Van Buren, 2020). Finally, management and accounting research has identified trends in non-financial reporting and disclosure requirements (Hubers & Thijssens, 2023; Kamminga, 2016; Leite et al., 2024; Tsalis et al., 2023). Despite the different perspectives adopted to study the phenomenon, research on HRDD remains fragmented and inconsistent. There are still significant gaps in relation to HRDD, particularly from an economic and business perspective. Most

I. Mastrorocco, *From Voluntary Responsibility to Regulatory Compliance*, SIDREA Series in Accounting and Business Administration,
https://doi.org/10.1007/978-3-032-34492-2_2

research takes a normative approach, while only a few studies have linked HRDD to aspects such as corporate governance, supply chain management, and management practices (Di Lorenzo, 2018; Hofmann et al., 2018; Kach et al., 2024; Parella, 2019). Furthermore, several papers criticise the adoption of this practice as purely symbolic with no real substantive application (Edelman, 2016; Rogerson et al., 2024). This criticism led to a debate about the advantages and limitations of voluntary versus binding regulations (Hamm, 2022). This debate intensified after the European Commission launched the CSDDD proposal in 2022, which was then approved in 2024 and will come into full force in the coming years (Kiewisch, 2025; Smit et al., 2020). This measure appears to be quite ambitious and aims to create a new framework for corporate governance and corporate responsibility at the European level. However, there are still several doubts about its implementation and the risk of it becoming a tick-the-box exercise (Deva et al., 2023; Leite et al., 2024). As it is a recently implemented measure, there is a lack of systematic analysis linking the development of the concept of HRDD with its application in the context of binding rules.

Despite growing interest in this topic, there have been few systematic attempts to map the literature within the business and management context. Notably, two literature reviews have been published on this topic: one by Rasche and Waddock (2021), analysing the evolution of literature on the UNGPs within the CSR research field and introducing the concept of due diligence, and another by Dempere et al. (2024), examining the impact of the CSDDD on businesses from an entrepreneurial perspective. However, to date, no study provides a systematic mapping of HRDD from managerial and economic perspectives or integrates a static analysis of the current state of research on HRDD with a dynamic analysis of expected regulatory changes.

This study, therefore, aims to address these gaps by conducting an SLR that incorporates bibliometric analyses of HRDD in business, management, and accounting. The review will focus specifically on the transition from voluntary to mandatory due diligence and its implications for corporate behaviour. Specifically, the study answers the following general research question:

What is the current state of the debate on HRDD in management and accounting? What are the main research gaps and avenues for future research?

The aim of the study is not only to summarise the existing, but also to interpret it from an economic and managerial perspective, and to address this less-discussed area in the field of BHR. In addition, the study makes an innovative contribution by establishing a link between management literature and regulatory measures. The study is one of the first contributions to systematically analyse the topic of HRDD, particularly concerning the introduction of CSDDD. In this way, the study makes a twofold contribution. From a theoretical perspective, it defines the existing research framework on HRDD and highlights the opportunities and disadvantages of CSDDD (Dupont et al., 2024). It also identifies research gaps and ideas for future research, which are addressed in the following chapters. From a practical perspective, the study outlines the challenges and opportunities for management in implementing

HRDD, especially after the entry into force of binding regulations, and ultimately provides useful insights for policymakers and other stakeholders.

The rest of the chapter is organised as follows. Section 2.2 explains the research methodology, while Sect. 2.3 presents the descriptive analyses of the selected articles. Section 2.4 defines the main themes of the articles analysed, while Sect. 2.5 discusses research gaps and potential questions for future research. Finally, the conclusions are presented in the sixth section.

2.2 Research Methodology

Building on the increasing academic attention to HRDD within the broader BHR debate, this chapter uses a systematic literature review to show how the concept has been specifically addressed in business and management research. The focus is on identifying the extent and way HRDD has been explored in empirical and theoretical contributions, to clarify existing approaches and highlight potential research opportunities. It is one of the most effective techniques for analysing all contributions to a specific topic in a comprehensive manner. As defined by Kraus et al. (2020) an SLR "is a review of an existing body of literature that follows a transparent and reproducible methodology in searching, assessing its quality and synthesising it, with a high level of objectivity". Furthermore, this methodology minimises the potential bias in selecting and analysing articles (Webster & Watson, 2002). This chapter combines two complementary methodological approaches: a systematic literature review following PRISMA guidelines for selecting and analysing articles, and a bibliometric analysis using VOSviewer and the keyword co-occurrence technique to identify thematic clusters and research trends. This combination is a common approach in literature reviews, providing both an analytical overview and a critical discussion (Mukhtar et al., 2025).

Specifically, the first step of the systematic literature review is to define specific research questions that define the scope and guide the following steps. The research questions derived from the general aim of the chapter are as follows:

1. *What is the current state of the art in research about HRDD?*
2. *What analytical approaches and thematic trends have emerged in the academic literature on HRDD in the business context?*
3. *What are the expected evolutions after the introduction of mandatory regulations?*
4. *What are the main research gaps and avenues for future research?*

The first research question is oriented towards defining the state of the art of the scientific debate on HRDD in the disciplines of economics, management, and accounting. To answer this question, a descriptive analysis of the selected studies is presented, including an assessment of their main characteristics, such as authors, journals, citations, temporal, and geographical distribution. The second research question aims instead to discuss the modus operandi of the authors dealing with the topic of HRDD. Specifically, it aims to observe which methodological and conceptual approaches the authors adopt. The third research question is more timely and aims to observe how the topic of HRDD has evolved and to understand the role of regulation, in particular of the CSDDD. The final research question aims to explore aspects that the authors have not addressed previously but may offer insights for future research.

After defining the research questions, the second step in the research protocol of an SLR involves defining the analysis sample. The methodology to perform this systematic review is based on the PRISMA ("preferred reporting items for systematic reviews and meta-analyses") Protocol for selecting and analysing articles. This protocol appears to be particularly useful for minimising bias in sample selection and analysis by providing explicit and systematic methods in advance (Cochrane, 2021; Patterson, 2024; Szablewska & Kubacki, 2023).

The search was conducted using two of the most widely adopted article databases: Scopus and EBSCO. Scopus was selected for its extensive coverage of peer-reviewed articles in the social sciences, economics, and management, and for its bibliometric features. EBSCO, on the other hand, was selected as a complementary source. The exclusion of Web of Science is supported by Lombardi and Secundo (2021), who demonstrated a high degree of overlap between this platform and Scopus in the social sciences. The research is based solely on an analysis of the topic of HRDD from an economic, managerial, and accounting perspective, for which the following research areas were selected: "Business, management and accounting" and "Economics, econometrics and finance", while academic sources/journals with a predominantly legal focus were removed from the list. Peer-reviewed articles, book chapters, and reviews in English were selected. No time limits were applied to observe the entire evolution of the HRDD topic.

Based on the described criteria, articles were collected in the following steps. First, a search string was made that was applied to Scopus: TITLE-ABS-KEY (busines* OR corporat* AND "human rights" OR "modern slavery" OR "labour rights") AND TITLE-ABS-KEY (due AND diligence OR hrdd) and EBSCO: (business or corporate and human rights) AND due diligence.

After applying the search strings, 512 documents from Scopus and 1113 from EBSCO were obtained. After applying the selected filters and eliminating duplicates, the sample was composed of 168 articles from Scopus and 103 from EBSCO. By eliminating publications not in line with the topic of analysis based on the type of publication, language, and content, based on the title, source, and abstract, the following articles were found: 103 from Scopus and 23 from EBSCO. Following the analysis of the articles by reading the entire text, further texts were eliminated because they were oriented towards the legal theme, or because they did not focus on companies but on countries, or because the source was not academically relevant. At the end of the screening process, the final sample of articles is composed of 89 (70 from Scopus and 19 from EBSCO). The analysis was performed between April and May 2025.

The sample selection and analysis procedure are shown in Fig. 2.1.

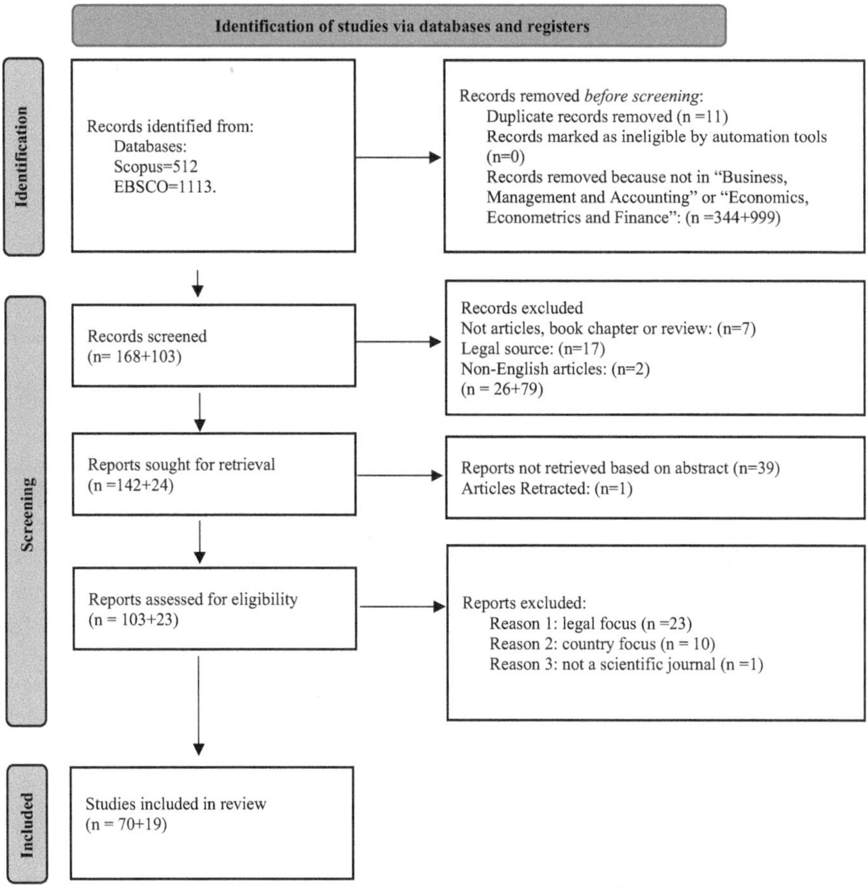

Fig. 2.1 PRISMA framework. *Source*: Author's own elaboration based on the PRISMA statement of Page et al. (2021)

The third step of the SLR is the analysis of the chapter. After obtaining the final list, all sources were added to a Microsoft Excel spreadsheet and evaluated according to different parameters (journal, year, geographical scope, citations, methodology, purpose of analysis, main results, discussions, and implications). Afterwards, the articles were subdivided and organised thematically to identify the different approaches adopted to analyse HRDD. The final step of the analysis is the presentation of results according to the research questions. The first part of the results consists of descriptive statistics of the analysed articles, including the representation of the time evolution of articles and citations, journals (journals with more articles and citations), articles (most cited articles), geographical distribution of authors, and adopted methodologies. The content analysis has been presented to describe the main thematic approaches used to delve into HRDD questions and explore the evolution of HRDD, as well as the introduction of mandatory regulations. Finally, research gaps and future advancements are presented.

2.3 Descriptive Analysis of the Articles

The main aim of this section is to present and describe the most important features of the articles analysed to answer the first research question (*What is the current state of the art in research about HRDD?*). Starting from the temporal evolution of the publications, the number of articles and the average number of citations for each year of the analysis are presented. The temporal representation can be seen in Fig. 2.2. Although any temporal constraints were not defined to fully analyse the phenomenon, the first articles on HRDD appeared in 2009, the year marked by the framework published by Ruggie. As also reported by Blanco Vizarreta and Betta (2022), the number of published articles increases from 2014, when only one article was published, to 2018, with seven articles. One of the possible reasons for this increasing trend can be attributed to the publication of the SDGs by the United Nations in 2015 and the increase in literature on non-financial reporting by companies in the field of management and accounting. After the COVID-19 pandemic, the number of published articles has increased again, with a maximum of 13 articles in 2024. This could be attributed to the increased attention due to recent regulatory developments, namely CSRD and CSDDD. Regarding the number of citations, it can be noted that most of the old articles were heavily cited as the main references in this area.

In this section, the development of publications according to the distribution of journals is presented. The articles included in the analysis were published in 46 different journals. The 15 most frequent journals, both in terms of the number of articles published and the number of citations, are shown in Fig. 2.3. The most important journal in this area is the *Business and Human Rights Journal*, in which 29 of the 89

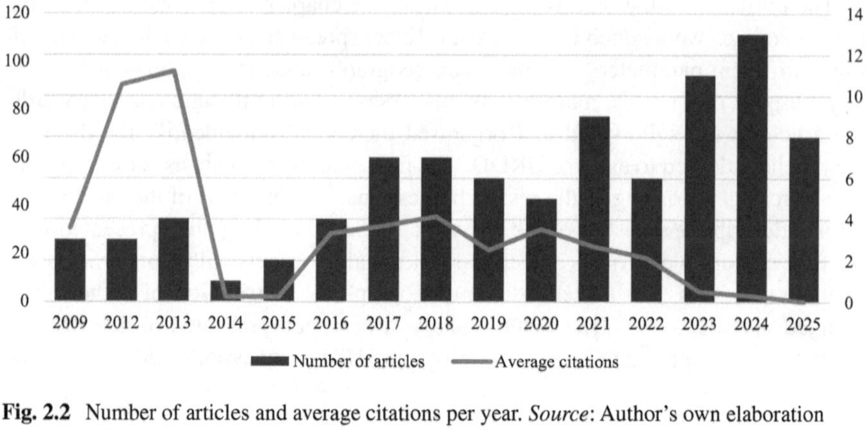

Fig. 2.2 Number of articles and average citations per year. *Source*: Author's own elaboration

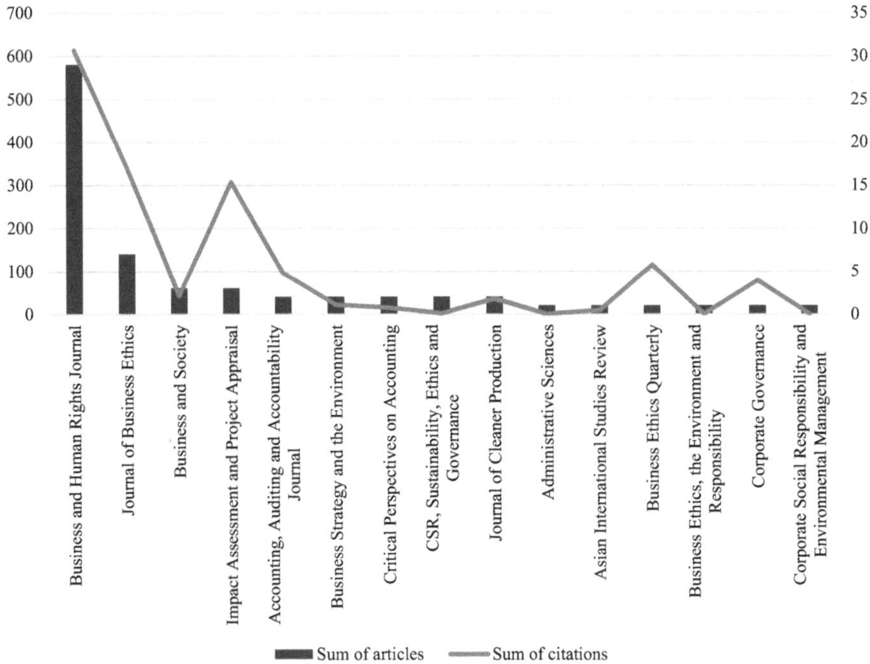

Fig. 2.3 Number of articles and citations per journal. *Source*: Author's own elaboration

articles were published and which was cited 613 times. This journal primarily deals with the topic of human rights from a business perspective and mainly presents theoretical and qualitative studies on this topic. It is followed by the *Journal of Business Ethics* with 7 articles and 342 citations, and *Business and Society*, as well as *Impact Assessment and Project Appraisal* with 3 articles each. The other journals, which all belong to the field of business, management, and economics, have between two and one publications.

Table 2.1 contains the list of the ten most cited articles, showing both the total number of citations achieved and the relative citations per year (CPY), which are obtained by dividing the total number of citations by the difference between the year of analysis (2025) and the year of publication of the respective article. The data comes from Scopus. The most cited article is "Human Rights and Impact Assessment: Clarifying the Connections in Practice" by Kemp and Vanclay (2013) with 224 citations, followed by "Conflict Minerals and Supply Chain Due Diligence: An Exploratory Study of Multi-tier Supply Chains" by Hofman et al. (2018), which has been cited 159 times so far. However, to get a more complete overview of the citation trend over time, it is essential to analyse the CPY. This is because some articles have been cited less because they are more recent. Analysing this additional metric shows that the article with the highest CPY is the one by Hofman et al. (2018), with 23 citations per year, compared to 19 for the article by Kemp and Vanclay (2013). These articles are considered the most influential in this context as they focus on

Table 2.1 The ten most-cited articles

Authors	Title	Year	Journal	Cited by	CPY	DOI
Kemp and Vanclay (2013)	Human rights and impact assessment: clarifying the connections in practice.	2013	Impact Assessment and Project Appraisal	224	19	https://doi.org/10.1080/14615517.2013.782978
Hofmann et al. (2018)	Conflict Minerals and Supply Chain Due Diligence: An Exploratory Study of Multi-tier Supply Chains	2018	Journal of Business Ethics	159	23	10.1007/s10551-015-2963-z
Cragg (2012)	Ethics, Enlightened Self-Interest, and the Corporate Responsibility to Respect Human Rights: A Critical Look at the Justificatory Foundations of the UN Framework	2012	Business Ethics Quarterly	148	11	10.5840/beq20122213
Muchlinski (2012).	Implementing the new UN corporate Human Rights Framework: Implications for corporate law, governance, and regulation	2012	Business Ethics Quarterly	115	9	10.5840/beq20122218
Macchi (2021)	The Climate Change Dimension of Business and Human Rights: The Gradual Consolidation of a Concept of 'Climate Due Diligence'	2020	Business and Human Rights Journal	87	17	https://doi.org/10.1017/bhj.2020.25
McCorquodale et al. (2017)	Human Rights Due Diligence in Law and Practice: Good Practices and Challenges for Business Enterprises	2017	Business and Human Rights Journal	81	10	10.1017/bhj.2017.2
Buhmann et al. (2019)	Do no harm and do more good too: connecting the SDGs with business and human rights and political CSR theory	2019	Corporate Governance (Bingley)	78	13	10.1108/CG-01-2018-0030
Fasterling and Demuijnck (2013)	Human Rights in the Void? Due Diligence in the UN Guiding Principles on Business and Human Rights	2013	Journal of Business Ethics	77	6	10.1007/s10551-013-1822-z
Graetz and Franks (2013)	Incorporating human rights into the corporate domain: due diligence, impact assessment and integrated risk management.	2013	Impact Assessment and Project Appraisal	57	5	https://doi.org/10.1080/14615517.2013.771006
Fasterling (2017)	Human Rights Due Diligence as Risk Management: Social Risk Versus Human Rights Risk	2017	Business and Human Rights Journal	54	7	10.1017/bhj.2016.26

Source: Author's own elaboration

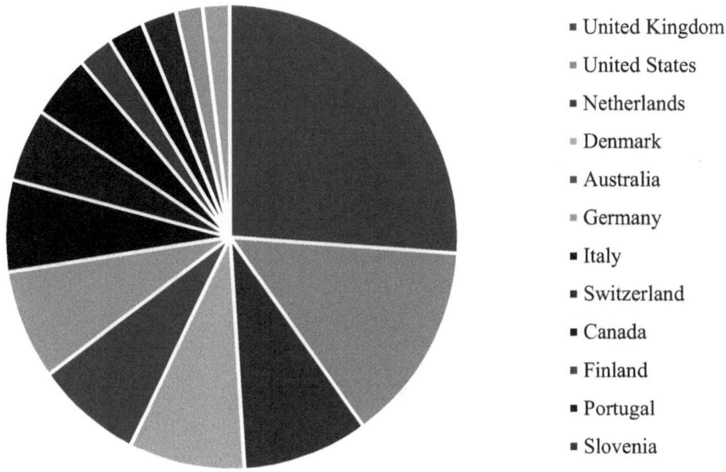

Fig. 2.4 Articles country distribution. *Source*: Author's own work

two of the most discussed aspects, namely the HRIA, which is considered part of HRDD, and conflict minerals, which are a hot topic in both academia and practical discussions on HRDD. The lowest level in terms of total number of citations in this table was by Fasterling (2017) with the article "Human Rights Due Diligence as Risk Management: Social Risk Versus Human Rights Risk", which was cited 54 times and has a CPY value of 7. The lowest level in terms of CPY has been reached by Graetz and Franks (2013) with the article "Incorporating Human Rights into the Corporate Domain: Due Diligence, Impact Assessment and Integrated Risk Management", which was cited 57 times and has a CPY of 5.

In this section, the descriptive statistics illustrate the cross-national distribution of the articles across the various countries (Fig. 2.4). More than a quarter (26%) of the articles were published in the United Kingdom, followed by the United States, where 14% of the articles in the sample were published. Similar rates were achieved by European countries such as the Netherlands (9% of the sample), Denmark (8%), Germany (8%), Italy (6%), and Switzerland (5%). In Australia, 8% of the sample was published. As can be seen, articles on HRDD are mainly published in developed countries in the Western world. In contrast, developing countries are only represented by Brazil, where only 2% of the sample was published, and Slovenia, with 3% of the total articles. These results illustrate that there is a large difference in the publication of articles between developed and developing countries, emphasising that human rights issues are not equally valued by all countries and scholars.

In the last section of the descriptive statistics, the articles have been clustered according to the chosen methodological approach to answer the first part of the second research question *(What analytical approaches and thematic trends have emerged in the academic literature on HRDD in the business context?*). Figure 2.5 shows that most of the articles (55% of the sample) analysed follow a theoretical and conceptual approach focusing on the description and conceptualisation of

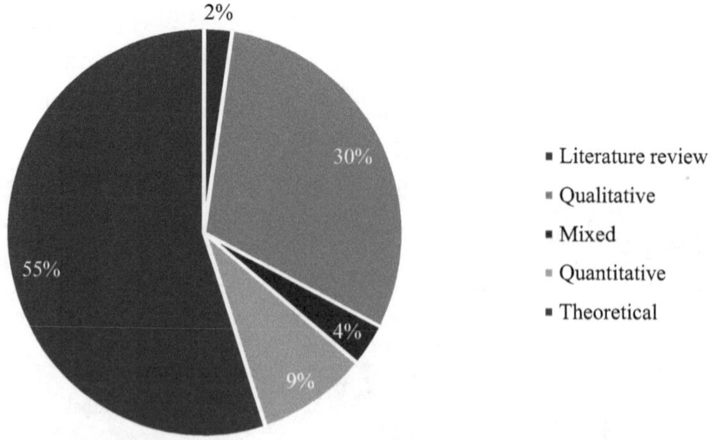

Fig. 2.5 Methodological approaches. *Source*: Author's own elaboration

HRDD, its main components, related practices, and its application in different contexts and sectors. The empirical works have been categorised into three types based on the data used: qualitative, quantitative, and mixed (qualitative and quantitative). The qualitative method is the most frequently used, as it accounts for 30% of the sample, while the quantitative method is used in only 9% of the articles, and the mixed method in 4% of the sample. Qualitative articles mostly use questionnaires, interviews, and case studies to evaluate the concept of HRDD, while quantitative articles mostly use secondary data and regression analyses, especially in the context of disclosure of non-financial information and sustainability issues. Finally, the literature review is barely represented in the sample, with only two articles. These are the literature reviews "The UN Guiding Principles on Business and Human Rights: Implications for Corporate Social Responsibility Research" by Rasche and Waddock (2021) and "The Entrepreneurial Impact of the European Directive on Corporate Sustainability Due Diligence" by Dempere et al. (2024). The low presence of reviews of previous literature is one of the reasons justifying the current review.

2.4 Thematic Analysis

In the next section, a thematic analysis of the selected articles was carried out to answer the second part of RQ2 *(What thematic trends have emerged in the academic literature on HRDD in the business context?)*. The articles were analysed for their main characteristics and then divided into five clusters according to their content (Nicolò et al., 2024). Articles were assigned to their respective clusters in a two-step process. Firstly, VOSviewer was used to analyse keyword co-occurrence, identifying thematic groups based on the frequency and proximity of keywords across the selected articles. Secondly, each cluster was manually reviewed

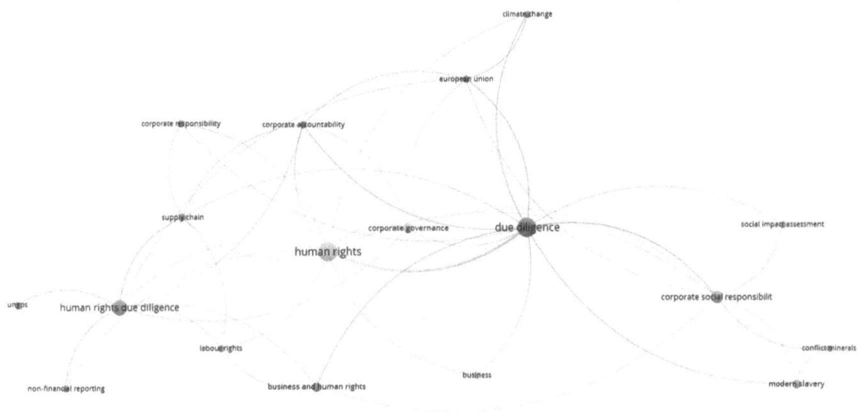

Fig. 2.6 Co-occurrence keywords representations. *Source*: Author's own elaboration

according to the title, abstract, and main contribution of each included article examined (Marzi et al., 2025). In cases of overlap, articles were assigned to the cluster that best reflected the research's main focus. Figure 2.6 shows the results of the co-occurrence analysis. Each node represents a keyword, with its size reflecting the frequency of occurrence across the selected articles. The proximity between nodes indicates the frequency with which keywords appear together in the same article, while the colour identifies the cluster to which each keyword belongs.

In Cluster 1, the most frequent terms are "due diligence (26 occurrences), "European Union", and "corporate accountability" (4), "climate change" (3). In cluster 2, the terms analysed are "corporate social responsibility" (10), "modern slavery" (5), "social impact assessment", and "conflict minerals" (3 occurrences). Cluster 3 is composed of the following keywords: "business and human rights" (6), "corporate responsibility and supply chain" (4), and "labour rights" (3). In Cluster 4, the most recurrent keyword is "human rights", cited 26 times, followed by "corporate governance", cited 7 times and "business" (4). Finally, Cluster 5 is composed of three keywords, "human rights and due diligence", "non-financial report" (3), and "UNGPs" (3). After a brainstorming session conducted by the author, the following five clusters emerged, as reported in Table 2.2.

Table 2.2 Clusterisation process

Clusters	Authors
Characteristics, application, improvements and criticisms of HRDD	Amengual M.; Mota R.; Rustler A. Cragg, Wesley Deva S.; Ramasastry A.; Wettstein F. Ebert, Isabel Esoimeme E.E. Fasciglione, Marco Fasterling B. Fasterling B.; Demuijnck G. Götzmann N. Graetz, Geordan Graf A.; Iff A. Hogan B.F.; Reyes J. Ivo Emanuilov Kach A.P.; Bhakoo V.; McGaughey F.; Boersma M.; Nolan J.; Lichtman S.M. Karp, D. J. Kemp, Deanna Krajewski M.; Tonstad K.; Wohltmann F. Kriebitz A.; Lütge C. Lichuma C.O. Litwin D. McCorquodale R.; Smit L.; Neely S.; Brooks R. McGaughey F.; Voss H.; Cullen H.; Davis M.C. Muswaka L. Nolan J.; Taylor L. Nolan Justine O'Brien C.M.; Dhanarajan S. Quijano G.; Lopez C. Salcito K.; Wielga M. Shavin C. Stein M.A.; Bantekas I. Van Buren H.J., III; Schrempf-Stirling J.; Westermann-Behaylo M. Chamebers, Rachel
Application of HRDD in specific sectors	Aizawa M.; Dos Santos D.C.; Seck S.L. Arni L.; Kermode Y.; Leitz C.; Seidler A. Baydas L. Boele and Crispin Buhmann K Buhmann K, Davaanyam, Otgontuya Di Lorenzo F. Elbel J.; Bose O'Reilly S.; Hrzic R. Ishida H.; Wada H. Kamminga M.T. Martha, Carolina Martin-Ortega O. Montgomery, Robert Nagaivska D.; Uvarova O. Rao, Madhura Slawotsky J. van der Ploeg L.; Vanclay F. Wahab A.A.B. Wörsdörfer M.

(continued)

Table 2.2 (continued)

Clusters	Authors
HRDD and supply chain management	Amato-Neto J.; Amato L.F. Barrientos S.; Bianchi L.; Berman C. Boersma M. Hofmann H.; Schleper M.C.; Blome C. Lundan S.M.; Muchlinski P. McCall-Smith K.; Rühmkorf A. Sarfaty G.A. Schleper M.C.; Blome C.; Stevenson M.; Thürer M.; Tusell I.
Relationships between HRDD and sustainability and non-financial reporting	Al-Shaer H.; Albitar K.; Hussainey K. Buhmann K. Buhmann K.; Jonsson J.; Fisker M. Buhmann Kari García-Sánchez I.-M.; Raimo N.; Vitolla F.; Aibar-Guzmán B. Guix M.; Lotfy M. Hamann R.; Sinha P.; Kapfudzaruwa F.; Schild C. Lopatta K.; Tideman S.A.; Scheil C.; Makarem N. Macchi C. Macchi, C. Macchi, Chiara Matthews L.; Silva M.E.; Figueiredo M.D.; Lai J.Y. McPhail K.; Ferguson J. Moussa T.; Allam A.; Elmarzouky M. Muchlinski P. Penttilä V.; den Hond F.; Fougère M.; Solitander N. Principale S. Rasche A.; Waddock S. Rogerson M. Rogerson M.; Scarpa F.; Snelson-Powell A. Torelli R.; Fiandrino S.; Scarpa F.
The implications of mHRDD and CSDDD	Bueno N.; Bernaz N.; Holly G.; Martin-Ortega O. Dempere J.; Udjo E.; Mattos P. Lafarre, Anne Leite E.; Koporcic N.; Markovic S. Malutan, D Mieszkowska, Jowita Shulman, Skylar Smit L.; Bright C.; Pietropaoli I.; Hughes-Jennett J.; Hood P.

Source: Author's own work

2.4.1 *Characteristics, Application, Improvements, and Criticisms of HRDD*

The literature on HRDD shows a solid conceptual and normative basis but also reveals considerable tensions in the implementation of these principles. Several authors (Krajewski et al., 2021; McCorquodale et al., 2017; Muswaka, 2014) emphasise the roots of HRDD in the UNGPs and the "Protect, Respect and Remedy" framework, supported by the OECD Guidelines as a source of practical guidance (Nolan & Taylor, 2009; Shavin, 2019). However, the degree to which companies internalise these standards is far from uniform: rather than enforcement, this often depends on companies' moral commitment (Fasterling & Demuijnck, 2013). This raises the crucial question of the effectiveness of voluntary adoption, particularly given the dynamic and context-specific nature of human rights abuses. In this context, some scholars argue in favour of a hybrid approach that combines binding regulation with cooperative engagement between states and companies (Fasciglione, 2020). Others see HRDD less as a compliance mechanism and more as a moral obligation shared by states and companies (Cragg, 2012). The literature further elaborates on the components and applications of HRDD, while highlighting the limitations of its current implementation. O'Brien and Dhanarajan (2016) emphasise the central role of adopting human rights policies, conducting HRIAs and reporting, three elements that are seen as fundamental to embedding human rights in corporate practice. Their analysis suggests that while progress has been made since the introduction of the UNGPs, particularly through regulatory interventions, reporting standards, and the involvement of trade unions, the pace of change remains slow, as Karp (2023) also notes. This observation is in line with the general concern in this area about the gap between formal commitment and actual practice.

A more focused strand of research has looked at HRIA as a specific component of HRDD. Here, scholars agree that HRIA serves as a key mechanism for the integration of human rights into everyday corporate life (Götzmann, 2017; Graetz & Franks, 2013; Hogan & Reyes, 2023; Kemp & Vanclay, 2013; Salcito & Wielga, 2018). However, the contexts in which these assessments are conducted can radically change their scope and relevance. Graf and Iff (2017), for example, broaden the discussion by considering conflict-affected areas and argue that conventional HRIA frameworks are inadequate if they are not complemented by conflict analysis.

Finally, some contributions emphasise the role of external pressures in shaping HRDD practices. Amengual et al. (2023) and Stein and Bantekas (2021) show how multinational companies, especially those under heavy public scrutiny, are strongly influenced by what Amengual et al. (2023) refer to as the "court of public opinion". From this perspective, reputational risks and stakeholder perceptions become just as relevant as legal or regulatory frameworks when it comes to persuading companies to adopt HRDD and related soft law instruments.

Another strand of literature narrows down the scope of HRDD by analysing specific human rights concerns. Stein and Bantekas (2021) argue for "disability-inclusive HRDD" and point to the persistent marginalisation of persons with disabilities in international legal instruments. Similarly, Litwin (2023) extends the concept to economic inequality and suggests that companies should introduce due diligence processes specifically designed to identify and address inequality-related impacts. In contrast, Van Buren et al. (2021) question the ability of due diligence to effectively combat human trafficking within supply chains and express more general doubts about the limitations of HRDD as a practical solution. These debates overlap with a more general concern regarding the conceptualisation of HRDD itself. Several authors note that, despite different interpretations, HRDD is still largely treated as a risk management tool tied to legal liability (Fasterling, 2017; Quijano & Lopez, 2021). Such framing risks obscuring the normative basis of human rights protection. Nolan (2022) also warns that while social due diligence is advocated in the UNGPs, it remains underdeveloped and undermines a holistic approach. Scholars also emphasise the danger of symbolic compliance, where companies adopt tick-box measures without ensuring substantive engagement with rights holders (Deva et al., 2023; Quijano & Lopez, 2021).

In parallel, there is work looking at modern slavery, an issue closely linked to HRDD, particularly following legislative initiatives such as the UK Modern Slavery Act. Studies in this area highlight the inadequacy of current corporate practices; while regulation has advanced, companies remain reluctant to implement robust risk assessment and remediation mechanisms, the very measures that are most urgently needed to combat abuses (Esoimeme, 2020; Kach et al., 2024; McGaughey et al., 2022). These contributions thus highlight a recurring paradox: HRDD is increasing in scope and visibility, yet its operationalisation is often insufficient to address the most urgent and systemic human rights violations.

A final group of papers explores how HRDD interacts with the challenges of digitalisation and Industry 4.0. Ebert et al. (2021) present the protection of privacy as a human right and introduce the idea of "privacy due diligence" in response to new forms of labour and data-driven business models. Emanuilov and Yordanova (2022) propose a decentralised, collaborative approach to HRDD that is tailored to the context of smart manufacturing and thus extends due diligence beyond the traditional company-centric perspective. Kriebitz and Lütge (2020) also emphasise the human rights risks associated with artificial intelligence (AI) and call for preventive measures to ensure that the use of these technologies does not lead to new forms of harm. Overall, these studies emphasise the adaptability of HRDD but also highlight the increasing complexity of embedding human rights safeguards in rapidly evolving technological environments. Taken together, the literature reviewed in this first cluster demonstrates both the conceptual richness and the persistent ambiguities surrounding HRDD.

2.4.2 Application of HRDD in Specific Sectors

A significant body of literature applies HRDD to high-risk sectors, with mining receiving particular attention due to its history of human rights abuses. Scholars emphasise both the necessity and the challenges of implementing HRDD in this context. Structural barriers such as limited transparency, complex value chains, and financial constraints often hinder effective due diligence. To address these issues, Aizawa et al. (2018) argue for supportive legal and financial frameworks, including tax incentives, social impact bonds and early equity programmes, while Buhmann (2017, 2023) highlights the potential to turn human rights and environmental concerns into opportunities for local development, provided that robust regulatory instruments, such as the OECD Guidelines or China's Due Diligence Guidance for Responsible Mineral Supply Chains (CCMC), are used effectively. Other contributions focus on operational mechanisms. Boele and Crispin (2013) propose an HRIA framework tailored to the sector and emphasise the importance of education and training in building a culture of risk identification and management. Similarly, Elbel et al. (2023), examining artisanal cobalt mining in the Democratic Republic of Congo, show that while CSDDD can lead to positive outcomes, its effectiveness is constrained by the geopolitical environment and limited participation of affected communities. This emphasises the importance of including victims' voices in policymaking.

Other articles included in this cluster adopt a case-based perspective to show how HRDD can be both a compliance tool and a source of long-term value creation. Martha and Logahan (2016), examining BP's Tanggu project in Papua, illustrate how the company's neglect of HRDD exposed it to criticism from NGOs and damaged its reputation, underpinning the argument that incorporating human rights considerations is not only a moral obligation but also a prerequisite for sustainable business success. Similarly, Di Lorenzo (2018) points to public-private partnerships as a means to strengthen collaboration, improve supply chain management, and promote co-creation of value.

In addition to mining, several other sectors have been identified as particularly vulnerable to human rights risks, each posing different challenges for HRDD. The defence industry is under constant stakeholder scrutiny, which creates a strong moral imperative for compliance with the UNGPs. However, as Baydas (2025) notes, companies often adopt HRDD not only for ethical reasons but also to mitigate legal, financial, and reputational risks or to gain a competitive advantage. Kamminga (2016) shows that companies facing frequent allegations of human rights violations tend to use HRDD primarily to protect their reputation. Nagaivska and Uvarova (2024) argue that in conflict-affected environments, standard due diligence is insufficient and propose the concept of "heightened HRDD" (hHRDD), which takes into account context-specific concerns such as workers' health and safety, mental health, and the treatment of vulnerable groups.

While the financial sector is not directly linked to human rights abuses, it plays a crucial direct role through investment and lending decisions. Arni et al. (2015) use the example of UBS to show how banks can contribute to the mainstreaming of HRDD by integrating it into internal processes and supporting initiatives such as the Thun Group. However, Wörsdörfer (2015) points out significant shortcomings of this initiative, including a narrow focus on the second pillar of the UNGP, limited attention to reporting and tracking, and insufficient stakeholder dialogue. Despite these limitations, it represents an important starting point for mainstreaming HRDD in financial institutions. Similarly, Davaanyam and Krajewski (2025) emphasise that financial actors should not only avoid negative impacts but also actively support the SDGs through their investment decisions.

The food industry also proves to be a critical sector. Wahab (2020), who analyses palm oil production, shows that despite the increasing introduction of strategies and due diligence obligations, weak regulatory frameworks, scarce resources, and heterogeneous market pressure limit the effectiveness of HRDD. Rao et al. (2024) take this discussion further by proposing a due diligence framework for the food sector based on the UNGPs, the SDGs, and the CSDDD. They emphasise how this approach differs from voluntary CSR by embedding binding human rights obligations into supply chain governance.

Finally, specific contexts also shed light on the scope and adaptability of HRDD. Ishida and Wada (2017), focusing on the 2020 Tokyo Olympics, show how major sporting events bring with them an increased risk of human rights violations and require proactive institutional measures. Martin-Ortega (2018) highlights procurement contracts in the electronics sector as a promising tool for embedding HRDD in supply chain management, linking contractual obligations with human rights safeguards.

In contrast, Slawotsky (2023) shows how companies can use procurement contracts to increase the responsiveness of states to human rights concerns. Analysing Israel's failure to respect the right to informed consent during the COVID-19 vaccination campaign, the author argues that Pfizer should have leveraged its due diligence practices and prior experience to safeguard this right. Montgomery and Maggio (2009) also recognise the challenges of protecting workers' rights in large-scale projects and propose a methodology aligned with host and home country regulations as well as ILO conventions. Their framework combines due diligence and labour condition assessments with performance monitoring and best practices that extend beyond legal compliance. Similarly, van der Ploeg and Vanclay (2017) introduce the concept of the "human rights sphere", a seven-step process designed to prevent and address human rights impacts in large-scale projects through a rights-holder-centred approach. All these contributions underline the central role of procurement mechanisms and large-scale project management in embedding HRDD. They show that while regulatory alignment provides a baseline, meaningful protection of rights requires proactive leverage, continuous monitoring, and approaches that place affected communities at the core of corporate responsibility.

2.4.3 HRDD and Supply Chain Management

Numerous research papers address HRDD in the context of supply chain management, highlighting its potential and limitations. Amato-Neto and Amato (2019) analyse Brazilian companies and find that human rights disclosure in codes of conduct is low. They emphasise that consumer pressure, stakeholder engagement, and legal frameworks are the main drivers of greater transparency. Boersma (2018) also reiterates the central role of stakeholders, focusing on child labour and advocating multi-stakeholder initiatives—from audits and certification to remediation and holistic approaches—as effective mechanisms to address grievances related to due diligence. Nevertheless, the literature also identifies significant weaknesses in current practices. Sarfaty (2021), for example, highlights the shortcomings of external auditing, noting its limited ability to detect non-compliance, and calls for a reassessment of audit design and implementation. Hofmann et al. (2018), drawing on interviews, offer a broader perspective and demonstrate that supply chain due diligence (SCDD) can reduce reliance on conflict minerals and enhance rights protection. However, they also acknowledge that the effectiveness of SCDD depends on overcoming barriers and balancing costs and benefits. These concerns align with those of Schleper et al. (2022), who demonstrate that costs are unevenly distributed within supply chains, with upstream actors shouldering the greatest burden. Their study proposes remedies such as supplier capacity building, contractual incentives, certification, and technological innovations such as blockchain. The institutional environment also plays a crucial role. McCall-Smith and Rühmkorf (2019) link SCDD to a broader regulatory trend characterised by international frameworks such as the SDGs, CSR initiatives, the UNGPs, and the OECD Guidelines, as well as national laws such as the UK Modern Slavery Act and the US Dodd-Frank Act. In this environment, the second pillar of the UNGPs is often cited as both a soft law instrument and a public-private governance mechanism. Lundan and Muchlinski (2012) argue that this pillar requires companies to implement robust monitoring processes and ensure transparency in supplier relationships. Barrientos et al. (2019) support this view by showing how governance based on the UNGPs can also be used to reduce gender-based discrimination in global value chains and thus promote a gender-sensitive HRDD approach. Overall, the literature portrays supply chain HRDD as a necessary but unevenly implemented mechanism.

2.4.4 Relationships Between HRDD and Sustainability and Non-financial Reporting

Another part of the literature examines the interaction between HRDD, CSR, and sustainability reporting and identifies both complementarities and tensions. Buhmann et al. (2019) emphasise the institutional foundations of this relationship in the SDGs, which enable companies to extend due diligence beyond the negative obligation to "do no harm" to the positive responsibility to "do more good". This broader framework not only strengthens the UNGPs but also increases the legitimacy of companies. Building on this, several scholars argue in favour of a holistic approach to HRDD that incorporates the environmental and climate change dimensions. Macchi (2021) and Macchi and Bernaz (2021) argue that environmental protection must be recognised as a fundamental human right and that companies are, therefore, obliged to integrate environmental aspects into oversight, reporting, and communication systems. Matthews et al. (2025) apply this perspective to supply chains and suggest that HRDD can serve as a bridge between human rights and environmental justice by extending corporate accountability to environmental impacts. The complementarity between CSR and HRDD is further explored by Rasche and Waddock (2021), who argue that, despite their differences, binding

UNGP principles versus voluntary CSR, both approaches can jointly advance HRDD practices by clarifying the roles and responsibilities of different stakeholders. Empirical support for this link is provided by Al-Shaer et al. (2024), who find that sustainability-oriented governance factors such as external audits and sustainability committees play a crucial role in promoting the disclosure of due diligence for conflict materials. The role of reporting and communication is another key concern. Although often considered secondary to implementation, reporting is a central pillar of the HRDD. While the 2014 Non-Financial Reporting Directive (NFRD) requires disclosure of information on sustainability and human rights, its focus remains on compliance and accountability. In contrast, HRDD communication under the UNGPs is more preventative and requires both ex-post reporting of results and ex-ante disclosure of risks and mitigation strategies. From this perspective, reporting becomes a proactive and continuous process that requires meaningful stakeholder engagement to identify and address risks before violations occur (Buhmann, 2018). Although international guidelines exist, human rights disclosure remains poorly defined and inconsistently implemented. Companies often rely on non-binding agreements, and the challenges are particularly acute for SMEs (McPhail & Ferguson, 2016). To address these gaps, Muchlinski (2012) calls for a shift from a shareholder-centred to a stakeholder-centred model and advocates the idea of the "civil corporation", where employees and other stakeholders are fully involved in decision-making processes.

Empirical research on human rights disclosure is limited, but it provides important insights. García-Sánchez et al. (2025) show that companies with people-centred governance structures disclose more information on compliance with human and labour rights. In contrast, Guix and Lotfy (2025) find in their analysis of the hotel sector that while companies report on modern slavery as part of due diligence and risk management, disclosure often varies between symbolic and substantive approaches, depending on characteristics such as company size and ownership. Rogerson et al. (2024), drawing on Oliver's (1991) framework, also find that corporate disclosure in Europe is more conversation-oriented than action-oriented, while Moussa et al. (2023) confirm that companies provide symbolic information about modern slavery but are less transparent about substantive issues such as KPIs, training, and remediation. Interestingly, their study also shows that gender diversity on boards correlates with higher levels of disclosure, which is consistent with gender socialisation theory. Institutional theory has been widely used to explain the determinants of disclosure. Hamann et al. (2009) show that in South Africa, contrary to expectations, neither industry sensitivity nor company size has a significant impact on HRDD disclosure; instead, institutional and financial market pressures together with internal strategies and management commitment are the most important factors. Similarly, Lopatta et al. (2023) find that Fortune 500 companies disclose relatively little on human rights compared to other sustainability issues, but disclosure increases with visibility, industry sensitivity, and institutional pressure. In the Russian context, Rogerson et al. (2024) confirms a generally low level of disclosure, although companies listed on foreign markets tend to show greater openness, reflecting the influence of cross-border institutional pressure. Finally, the governance structures themselves also prove to be important determinants. Both Principale (2023) and Torelli et al. (2024) show that board size, board diversity, CSR committees, and the separation of the roles of CEO and chair have a positive influence on HRDD, while board independence has little impact. Torelli et al. (2024) also find that the national institutional context is less significant for disclosure practices than differences at the industry level.

Overall, this literature reveals a persistent discrepancy between symbolic and substantive disclosure of HRDD. While governance mechanisms, institutional pressure, and stakeholder engagement can promote transparency, disclosure remains inconsistent and is often limited to formal statements rather than concrete actions.

2.4.5 The Implications of mHRDD and CSDDD

The last part of the literature deals with the development of HRDD in the context of state regulation, with a particular focus on CSDDD. Smit et al. (2020), comparing perceptions in the EU and the UK, show that respondents are dissatisfied with the current regulatory landscape and call for legal certainty and a harmonised EU standard. While stakeholders call for clearer rules to make it easier to exert influence, they also emphasise the importance of avoiding "tick-the-box" compliance. In a similar vein, Maluțan et al. (2024) describe the introduction of mandatory HRDD (mHRDD) laws at the EU level as potentially revolutionary, as they could overcome the weaknesses of fragmented national regulations. However, their analysis also emphasises the persistent doubts about the effectiveness of the Directive in actually reducing adverse human rights impacts, with corporate governance identified as a key mediating factor.

Empirical evidence underpins the role of binding interventions. Lafarre and Rombouts (2022), analysing the French experience, find that binding regulations have a positive impact on companies' human rights performance, suggesting that legal coercion can help close the gap between principle and practice. Other contributions trace the development of European legislation since the 2014 NFRD, which focused on disclosure but required companies to report on human rights risks along their value chains (Fasciglione, 2020; Lafarre & Rombouts, 2022; Shulman, 2024). Buhmann (2025) emphasises the increasing interconnectedness of reporting and due diligence, particularly with the CSRD and CSDDD, and argues that due diligence should not only provide compliance information but also create learning processes that strengthen both corporate decision-making and societal trust.

The literature also deals directly with the CSDDD and analyses its scope of application, its main features, and possible challenges in its implementation. Bueno et al. (2024) outline the main components of the Directive, its personal and material scope, and the obligations it imposes, while pointing out ambiguities that could hinder enforcement, including the definition of causation, the extent of responsibility in the value chain, and the application of penalties. Concerns are also raised about extraterritorial effects, as these could complicate relations between European companies and non-EU countries.

Leite et al. (2024) also emphasise the vagueness of the Directive and the risks of a "political CSR" dynamic where large companies shape the outcomes to their advantage. They warn that vague provisions could lead to "tick-the-box" compliance, while emphasising that the costs of implementation and maintenance could undermine competitiveness both within Europe and internationally. Dempere et al. (2024), conducting a literature review, recognise these constraints but also cite opportunities: in particular, the potential for long-term value creation through sustainable practices, improvements in ecosystem and supply chain management, and the development of collaborative networks with stakeholders. Other authors take a more critical stance. Mieszkowska (2024) warns that an unintended consequence could be the withdrawal of companies from high-risk regions, which would worsen the very conditions that the directive aims to improve. She also points to the uneven distribution of compliance costs along the value chain, which could disproportionately affect weaker suppliers. While acknowledging these challenges, Shulman (2024) emphasises the transformative ambition of the Directive, in particular the attempt to integrate human rights and environmental considerations into a single binding framework. These findings are central to the present research, which aims to explore how companies deal with these opportunities and challenges and whether the CSDDD can serve as a turning point in moving HRDD from voluntary rhetoric to mandatory, transformative practice.

2.5 Discussion

The analysis of thematic clusters and the associated content analysis enabled the creation of a comprehensive overview of HRDD in the research areas of business, management, and economics. These results enabled us to identify the most significant research gaps and provide insights into future developments in response to the fourth research question (RQ4): "*What are the most important research gaps and avenues for future research?*" The research gaps and future avenues for research are shown in Table 2.3.

Regarding the first group (characteristics, applications, improvements, and criticisms of HRDD), while many articles focus on the main activities that characterise HRDD or have developed alternative models relating to individual components of human rights, there is a lack of comprehensive overviews of their application in corporations. Furthermore, the methods used are primarily theoretical and/or conceptual, based on the evaluation of existing regulations and documents. By contrast, direct experience in the field is lacking, except in exceptional cases (Esoimeme, 2020; McCorquodale et al., 2017; McGaughey et al., 2022). Therefore, it is necessary to conduct empirical research based on the direct or indirect observation of corporate advocacy of human rights and the adoption of HRDD.

Table 2.3 Research gaps and future research questions

Cluster	Research gap	Future research questions
Characteristics, application, improvements and criticisms of HRDD	Failure to assess the sentiment of internal actors and the internal processes that affect HRDD. Poor level of empirical research with both primary and secondary data. Lack of studies assessing the actual outcome of HRDD in terms of reducing or eliminating human rights violations.	• *What are the managers' and decision makers' sentiments regarding HRDD?* • *What is the role of corporate actors in HRDD configuration and resource allocation related to this practice?* • *What are the main determining factors of HRDD? What are the main effects of HRDD?* • *Is HRDD implementation sufficient to reduce or eliminate human rights violations?*
Application of HRDD in specific sectors	Lack of empirical studies regarding the different impacts of voluntary industry guidelines and binding regulations. Failure to assess the role of financial, strategic and policy instruments in determining the application of HRDD and HRIA. Absence of analysis regarding the real determinants of HRDD, whether more strategic and reputational or moral.	• *What is the difference between the adoption of voluntary guidelines and binding regulations on HRDD in sectors with a high risk of human rights violations?* • *What role do legal, financial and political instruments play in the implementation of HRDD and HRIA?* • *What drives companies operating in high-risk sectors to implement HRDD? Strategic and reputational motivations or moral commitment?*
HRDD and supply chain management	Lack of focus on SMEs and the differences with larger companies within the supply chain. Failure to assess the potential role of digital technologies and artificial intelligence in HRDD.	• *How do SMEs perform HRDD in the supply chain context?* • *What is their role in the different phases that compose HRDD within the supply chain?* • *How do mimetic pressures shape the behaviour of SMEs in performing HRDD? How does HRDD change between large and small companies?* • *How does the introduction of artificial intelligence and blockchain technology influence HRDD?*

(continued)

Table 2.3 (continued)

Cluster	Research gap	Future research questions
Relationships between HRDD and sustainability and non-financial reporting	Failure to assess how HRDD reporting may evolve as a result of the new regulatory landscape (CSRD, ESRS and CSDDD).	• *Does the introduction of the ESRS standards improve the level and quality of disclosure concerning human rights and HRDD?* • *Does the level of reporting about HRDD confirm the actions taken by companies, or do they engage in cosmetic compliance?* • *Does the CSDDD reduce the gap between the disclosure of HRDD and the actual performance, or do companies adopt a "tick-the-box exercise"?*
The implications of mHRDD and CSDDD	Failure to assess the level of readiness of companies and comparison between as-is and to be scenarios. Lack of assessment of the potential impact of CSDDD on HRDD, reduction of cosmetic compliance and human rights violations. Absence of considerations on the role of corporate governance and the balance between the search for legitimacy and institutional pressures introduced by the CSDDD.	• *What is the impact of CSDDD implementation on HRDD practices in the European context?* • *What is the level of readiness of companies for the implementation of the directive?* • *Does the implementation of CSDDD reduce the level of cosmetic compliance?* • *Does the implementation of CSDDD increase the effectiveness of HRDD and the reduction of human rights violations?* • *How does corporate governance influence the implementation level of CSDDD?* • *How does the introduction of the CSDDD influence the adoption of human rights due diligence practices, and how do companies balance institutional compliance and legitimacy concerns?*

This makes it possible to understand the level of adoption of this practice in companies, and to identify which components receive more attention and resources, and which are less recognised. By collecting primary data through questionnaires or interviews, the attitudes of managers and decision-makers towards the implementation of HRDD can be understood, particularly in light of recent regulatory interventions (e.g. CSDDD). Furthermore, it will be possible to analyse the roles and responsibilities assigned to individuals, monitor the effectiveness of their actions, and propose corrective measures. Among the less recognised actors are intermediaries such as auditors and consultants, who can support companies, particularly with regard to the latest regulatory developments. Conversely, when collecting secondary data, indices can be constructed based on data provided by agencies and external actors (e.g. the World Benchmarking Alliance) that allow large-scale comparisons of the effectiveness and efficiency of due diligence in different contexts. Using these scores as dependent or independent variables in regression models allows the identification of the determinants of the introduction or effectiveness of HRDD, as well as the most important impacts on different dimensions (strategic, market, and organisational). It also enables the observation of the primary results of HRDD, such as whether and to what extent it leads to a reduction and/or elimination of human rights violations. This leads to the following research questions being proposed:

What are the managers' and decision makers' sentiments regarding HRDD?
What is the role of corporate actors in HRDD configuration and resource allocation related to this practice?
What are the main determining factors of HRDD? What are the main effects of HRDD?
Is HRDD implementation sufficient to reduce or eliminate human rights violations?

When analysing the second cluster (application of HRDD in specific sectors), several issues are identified, including an analysis of sectors most exposed to human rights violations, such as mining, extraction and defence. Some scenarios that do not relate to specific sectors are also identified, such as large-scale projects, which pose greater risks due to their characteristics. Consequently, however, several topics are under-researched, representing gaps in scientific research. In particular, it could be useful to compare the impact of existing guidelines for specific sectors and countries (e.g. CCMC), which are often applied voluntarily, with that of mandatory regulations. Another research gap concerns the role of legal, financial, and policy instruments introduced to support HRDD in different sectors. Although Aizawa et al. (2018) recognised these as important tools for overcoming barriers to the implementation of HRDD in the mining sector, there has been no empirical assessment of their impact. Therefore, future research could use case studies to explore how instruments such as social bonds, tax incentives and financing programmes can encourage companies to adopt HRIA and HRDD practices. In light of the public pressure on companies operating in high-risk sectors, it is also crucial to determine what motivates these companies to act: reputational and strategic considerations, or a moral obligation to defend human rights. In the event of human rights violations, reputational and legal damage can be severe and harm the company's future image.

Consequently, engagement in HRDD activities and related disclosure may be driven by opportunistic objectives rather than sincere interests. This raises concerns about social washing, whereby companies make public commitments to human rights to enhance their legitimacy without effecting substantive change. When HRDD becomes a symbolic tool used to manage external perceptions rather than a meaningful effort to address human rights risks, its transformative potential is undermined and superficial compliance practices are encouraged (Rogerson et al., 2024). In light of the research gaps that have been exposed, the following research questions are presented:

What is the difference between the adoption of voluntary guidelines and binding regulations on HRDD in sectors with a high risk of human rights violations?

What role do legal, financial and political instruments play in the implementation of HRDD and HRIA?

What drives companies operating in high-risk sectors to implement HRDD? Strategic and reputational motivations or moral commitment?

Regarding the third cluster (HRDD and supply chain management), the reviewed literature presents various global scenarios that predominantly concern large companies operating in multiple countries. However, an assessment of SMEs is crucial, particularly with regard to the challenges they face within supply chains. Large brands often rely on numerous small suppliers based in developing countries. Although some studies acknowledge the importance of these suppliers, the analysis of this segment remains poorly structured (Elbel et al., 2023; Wilhelm, 2024). Consequently, the lack of attention given to these actors hinders a comprehensive understanding of the HRDD context with regard to supply chain management.

Given the cost and complexity of HRDD-related activities, it is clear that SMEs are at a disadvantage compared to larger companies. Nevertheless, despite their limited size, SMEs can be directly or indirectly involved in incidents related to human rights violations. Given these limitations, it is essential to develop dedicated research into human rights abuses in global supply chains that considers the role of these actors. This analysis should consider the specific characteristics of SMEs, which not only face financial constraints, but also structural, organisational and cultural challenges. Furthermore, while these companies are often excluded from regulatory interventions such as the CSDDD, they are nevertheless indirectly affected by these changes and may adopt such practices under mimetic pressure (Leite et al., 2024). A second limitation is the lack of focus on power dynamics within the value chain. Finally, a third limitation is the absence of HRDD-related KPIs to measure effectiveness and efficiency in the supply chain. Although Schleper et al. (2022) cited some of these aspects concerning cost allocation, they need to be further developed to assess the power and risks of relationships within the global value chain.

Future research could address these shortcomings and propose solutions to the problems identified by the authors. In particular, AI and blockchain technologies could play a significant role in the supply chain. The introduction of digital technologies is already transforming this field in various contexts (Kriebitz & Lütge, 2020). Therefore, we anticipate research investigating whether adopting these technologies can mitigate human rights violations and improve the efficiency and effectiveness of HRDD. The following research questions are presented:

How do SMEs perform HRDD in the supply chain context?
What is their role in the different phases that compose HRDD within the supply chain?
How do mimetic pressures shape the behaviour of SMEs in performing HRDD? How does HRDD change between large and small companies?
How does the introduction of artificial intelligence and blockchain technology influence HRDD?

The fourth cluster, "Relationships between HRDD and sustainability and non-financial reporting", illustrates the identified connection between HRDD and sustainability. This is then translated into an assessment of HRDD disclosure in sustainability reports. This area of research is one of the most widely discussed, given that the debate between human rights and CSR is ongoing and particularly relevant. Furthermore, the recent Directive recognises the intrinsic relationship between the two, identifying both human rights and environmental protection as fundamental elements of sustainability to which due diligence relates. Despite the abundance of contributions on this topic, certain issues remain unaddressed. In light of the CSRD and the introduction of European Sustainability Reporting Standards (ESRS), it is important to assess how companies are implementing human rights disclosure under the new rules in the European context. Furthermore, many contributions cite companies' purely symbolic disclosure of HRDD and consequently show low focus on concrete actions. In this context, it would be interesting to observe the extent to which declarations correspond to actual performance in this area. This would highlight strategies based on "tick-the-box" exercises and cosmetic compliance. It would also encourage policymakers to promote initiatives that ensure the effective protection of human rights by companies. However, assessing these issues can be challenging due to limited transparency and access to information, as well as the omission of negative events. However, the CSDDD increases investigative opportunities by mandating oversight from national authorities and enabling stakeholders to evaluate compliance more effectively. In this context, the proposed research questions are as follows:

Does the introduction of the ESRS standards improve the level and quality of disclosure concerning human rights and HRDD?
Does the level of reporting about HRDD confirm the actions taken by companies, or do they engage in cosmetic compliance?
Does the CSDDD reduce the gap between the disclosure of HRDD and the actual performance, or do companies adopt a "tick-the-box exercise"?

The final cluster analysed (The Implications of MHRDD and CSDDD) examines the role of regulations that mandate the introduction of HRDD and focuses on contributions that explore the role and expectations surrounding the introduction of CSDDD. Although the directive is not yet in force, contributions in the analysed literature express scepticism about its implementation, mainly due to the expected high costs and disadvantages for European companies compared to their competitors. In light of these considerations, it is crucial to assess the willingness of European companies to implement the directive. Analysing the current state of practice in this area using primary and secondary data would make it possible to determine the current state and compare it with the target state. Once the Directive is in force, it will be necessary to assess its implementation and compare it with the target scenario in order to evaluate its success and propose corrective measures to policymakers. Such an analysis should primarily aim to determine whether and to what extent compliance with cosmetic remedies has decreased, and whether companies are more committed to reducing and/or eliminating human rights violations. Additionally, corporate governance is an important factor to analyse. This consists of internal actors, such as the board of directors, as well as external factors, such as auditors and consultants. These actors play a key role in determining the resources and activities allocated to HRDD and its results. Finally, it is necessary to understand how companies balance the obligation to comply with the need to legitimise. This provides important insight into the potential mismatch between the formal adoption of HRDD and its actual implementation, as well as how companies respond to institutional pressure.

What is the impact of CSDDD implementation on HRDD practices in the European context?
What is the level of readiness of companies for the implementation of the directive?
Does the implementation of CSDDD reduce the level of cosmetic compliance and increase the effectiveness of HRDD and the reduction of human rights violations?
How does corporate governance influence the implementation level of CSDDD?
How does the introduction of the CSDDD influence the adoption of human rights due diligence practices, and how do companies balance institutional compliance and legitimacy concern?

2.6 Conclusions

This chapter presents a knowledge base related to HRDD in the fields of business, management and accounting, economics and econometrics, and finance as a starting point for achieving the objectives of the entire dissertation. By applying an SRL and the PRISMA protocol to the Scopus and EBSCO databases, it was possible to analyse 89 articles, which were divided into five clusters that form a summary framework for HRDD. The analysis revealed several trends in the literature, including a preference for theoretical rather than empirical studies and a greater use of qualitative rather than quantitative analyses. In terms of content, many articles were found to take a descriptive approach, outlining the key points of HRDD based on regulatory measures such as the UNGPs and OECD guidelines, or observing this phenomenon in specific sectors or contexts. A much-discussed topic is also the evolution of HRDD in the context of increasingly internationalised supply chain management and the complex mechanism linking HRDD to sustainability and non-financial reporting issues. In this context, it is possible to include research that outlines how and whether HRDD practices have evolved thanks to the introduction of mandatory or non-mandatory regulatory interventions, with a particular focus on the entry into force of the CSDDD. This element is not only one of the focal points of the entire dissertation, but also a starting point for understanding the future impact of the Directive on corporate behaviour and the adoption of HRDD practices. A critical review of the current literature reveals several key observations. Firstly, while the predominance of theoretical and qualitative studies demonstrates the complexity of HRDD, it also indicates a reluctance to empirically assess the effectiveness of due diligence systems. This aspect appears crucial in light of the introduction of the CSDDD. Secondly, the high concentration of publications in Western countries, compared with the exclusion of those in developing countries, carries the risk of developing theoretically coherent frameworks that do not apply to the contexts in which violations occur. Thirdly, while several contributions to the literature highlight the symbolic nature of HRDD, there is an increasing need to develop methodologies and tools that can distinguish genuine implementation from cosmetic compliance.

Therefore, the results obtained through this systematic analysis thus offer several contributions for the further development of the literature. In particular, the chapter is one of the first studies to analyse the topic of HRDD from an economic and business perspective, going beyond the legal dimension. Secondly, the descriptive analysis, which comprises the first part of the chapter, makes it possible to observe both temporal and geographical trends and to identify the journals and authors that deal with these topics the most. The thematic and content analysis, on the other hand, reveals the most frequently covered research trends and thus serves as a basis for the development of future research. Similarly, the existence of research gaps and guidelines for future developments is a starting point for a more in-depth exploration of HRDD from different perspectives. The present chapter establishes the foundation for the subsequent chapters in two specific ways. First, the five thematic clusters identified through the systematic and bibliometric analysis define the conceptual boundaries of the HRDD debate and reveal the theoretical gaps that the following chapters aim to address. Second, the research questions proposed at the end of each cluster directly inform the agenda of Chaps. 3 and 4, which test the anticipatory impact of the CSDDD on corporate HRDD practices and identify the institutional and legitimacy factors that drive adoption.

From a practical point of view, the study has implications for various stakeholders. Starting with companies, the study emphasises the changes that will be introduced following the implementation of the Directive, requiring them to rethink their internal processes to comply with obligations. To this end, the study presents various practical tools such as audits, multi-stakeholder initiatives, and procurement contracts to achieve these goals. In addition, the literature analysed points out the costs that will be incurred, particularly by smaller companies, in order to comply with the new international legal framework, while also highlighting the opportunities from which companies can benefit. The results of the analysis will be particularly useful for policymakers as they will allow them to define the starting point for monitoring the impact of regulatory developments. In this respect, the analysis underlines the need to harmonise the rules in order to avoid fragmented and inconsistent application. In addition, it is essential to involve rights holders to ensure that the implementation of the Directive is not merely formal.

Despite its contributions, the chapter has some limitations. In particular, the analysis is based on only two databases, Scopus and EBSCO, and does not take into account other equally authoritative sources. Secondly, the author has chosen not to include working papers and conference proceedings, documents that have not been peer reviewed but may contain interesting contributions to the topic of the analysis. The same applies to works in languages other than English. As this is a constantly evolving topic, it is to be expected that the picture will be incomplete, especially in relation to the last cluster and thus to the implementation of the CSDDD. The articles outlining the Directive's role in global sustainable due diligence will likely be revised in the future.

Chapter 3
Explaining Corporate Behaviour in the Transition to Mandatory Due Diligence: An Institutional Theory Approach

3.1 Introduction

In recent years, the relationship between business and human rights has taken a central role in academic and political debate. At the heart of this debate is the concept of HRDD, a key mechanism for minimising the negative impact of business activities on human rights. Although this practice began as a voluntary tool, its application has been uneven and often limited to mere symbolic gestures (Wettstein, 2025). This has raised doubts about the effectiveness and efficiency of this instrument in ensuring corporate accountability (Hess, 2021). Against this backdrop, the introduction of the CSDDD represents a break with the past because, although there were national regulations dealing with HRDD, they appeared to be isolated cases and did not provide a consistent framework for the application of this practice (Butt & Kousar, 2024; Reinsberg & Steinert, 2025). It, therefore, represents a significant turning point not only for Europe, whose companies are directly involved in the transition from voluntary to mandatory due diligence, but also for foreign companies that have significant relations with Europe (Buhmann & Feld, 2024). In addition, a particular innovation introduced by the directive concerns the need for companies to be accountable for the responsibilities of actors along the supply chain, requiring them to broaden their horizons beyond their internal activities (Schilling-Vacaflor & Lenschow, 2023). While the application of the directive requires companies to make changes in terms of corporate governance, stakeholder relations, and supply chain management, it also presents several limitations, including operational costs, loss of competitiveness, and the risk of mere symbolic compliance without real substantive change (Leite et al., 2024). Given this starting point, which is still fragmented from both an academic and legal point of view, there is a need to develop a theoretical background that, based on the assumptions of institutional theory, defines the potential advantages and disadvantages of the directive and determines the potential response of companies to this legislation based on

I. Mastrorocco, *From Voluntary Responsibility to Regulatory Compliance*, SIDREA Series in Accounting and Business Administration,
https://doi.org/10.1007/978-3-032-34492-2_3

the different pressures to which they are exposed (Brammer et al., 2012; Rogerson et al., 2024; Wang et al., 2024). Specifically, this chapter, seeking to fill a gap in HRDD research, aims to answer the following research question:

RQ: How has HRDD evolved, and what is the institutional impact of the CSDDD on companies' practices?

To this end, this chapter presents a theoretical framework that conceptualises the evolution of HRDD between voluntary and binding dynamics, with a particular focus on the CSDDD and its peculiarities. Secondly, based on institutional theory, the framework highlights the opportunities and risks associated with this directive, while also providing potential solutions to minimise these risks. The contribution of this chapter is twofold. From a theoretical point of view, it is one of the first contributions to integrate economic and managerial perspectives with a framework of regulatory evolution in order to define the potential impact of this recent legal intervention. From a practical point of view, it offers useful implications for various stakeholders, including businesses, local communities, and policymakers, on how to address and take advantage of the new regulatory framework.

The rest of the chapter is organised as follows. Section 3.2 describes the main features of HRDD, while Sect. 3.3 outlines its integration into corporate practices and Sect. 3.4 illustrates the evolution of the related regulatory framework. Section 3.5 explores the adoption of HRDD according to different institutional pressures, while Sect. 3.6 assesses the potential impact of the directive. Finally, Sect. 3.7 sets out the conclusions.

3.2 The Emergence of Human Rights Due Diligence

HRDD has gained increasing attention following the introduction of Pillar II of the UN Guiding Principles on Business and Human Rights (UNGPs 17). According to these principles, companies must establish processes to identify, prevent, mitigate, and account for their human rights impact (Wettstein, 2021). From both BHR scholarship and a managerial standpoint, HRDD can be understood as a sensemaking process for three main reasons: interpreting and clarifying BHR obligations, identifying how business activities may lead to actual or potential adverse human rights impacts, and assessing how these impacts can be mitigated or prevented through corporate policies and practices (Olsen et al., 2025). The Office of the UN High Commissioner for Human Rights defines HRDD as an:

> Ongoing management process that a reasonable and prudent enterprise needs to undertake, in light of its circumstances (including sector, operating context, size, and similar factors) to meet its responsibility to respect human rights. (OHCHR, 2012, p. 4)

Based on this definition, HRDD encompasses several characteristics:

1. Continuous Process: HRDD is a continuous process that aims to identify risks that may have a negative impact on human rights rather than being a one-time event (Martin-Ortega, 2017; McCorquodale et al., 2017).
2. Structured Activities: According to Ramasastry (2015), HRDD is made up of a number of activities intended to accomplish three main objectives: identifying possible risks, preventing harm, and guaranteeing access to remedies.
3. Context-Dependent: Businesses can customise HRDD strategies according to their size and industry because the process can be adjusted to various business contexts. Because of the nature of their operations, some industries might need more standards and closer scrutiny (Li, 2022).
4. Two conflicting viewpoints influence HRDD: Mandatory human rights due diligence (mHRDD), which uses hard law tools to regulate HRDD, is an example of the first, duty-bearer perspective, which maintains that states are in charge of creating legal frameworks to protect human rights. Businesses are subject to particular legal obligations under domestic law, which provides clarity and predictability with regard to impact assessments, remediation, and human rights standards. The second viewpoint, known as the right-holder perspective, moves the emphasis from risks about the business to the effects on suppliers, customers, and distributors, among other stakeholders along the value chain.
5. Various Methods: Businesses can use a variety of HRDD strategies that fit with their operations. These consist of formal, independent HRDD procedures or incorporating HRDD into more extensive business management due diligence. The latter approach typically locates HRDD responsibilities within CSR or legal departments (McCorquodale et al., 2017).

HRDD includes several crucial tasks for businesses:

1. Human Rights Impact Assessment (HRIA): It looks at laws, policies, initiatives, and programmes to determine and quantify how they affect human rights. In the context of BHR, it is primarily used to assess the detrimental effects of business operations on the human rights of employees and community members, typically through ex-post evaluation (O'Brien & Dhanarajan, 2016). This phase encompasses desktop research, internal and external audits, investigations, reports from independent experts, and grievance procedures. The goal is to classify associated risks and evaluate the possible effects on stakeholders. At this point, leadership commitment is essential for recruitment, procurement, and resource allocation.
2. Reactions and Steps Taken: Businesses must incorporate the results of HRIA into their internal operations and take the necessary steps (UNGP 19). Budgeting for required interventions, offering training, enlisting human rights specialists, and putting contractual clauses like conduct codes or severing ties with partners who violate human rights are a few examples of possible actions. Determining how much a company should look into its business relationships and its level of accountability for the actions of third parties is still a major challenge, though (Lambooy, 2010).

3. Tracking Efficiency: Mechanisms for tracking and monitoring are crucial for evaluating how well HRDD measures are working. Businesses use benchmarking tools like the Corporate Human Rights Benchmark (CHRB) and the Global Reporting Initiative (GRI) to assess their performance and implement corrective measures.

3.3 The Challenges of Integrating HRDD into Corporate Activities

HRDD has its roots in traditional due diligence practices related to corporate governance. Historically, due diligence has evolved as a risk mitigation tool that focuses primarily on financial securities, key business transactions, and operational processes (Götzmann, 2017). It is closely linked to pre-contractual processes in mergers and acquisitions (Lambooy, 2010). However, there is no universally accepted definition of due diligence, and it is often described as a "container process" that involves the identification, assessment, and management of risks arising from business activities.

HRDD builds on this traditional concept and expands it by shifting the focus from protecting the company's interests to protecting individuals potentially affected by business activities. It represents a hybrid mechanism that combines corporate risk management practices with the state's duty to protect human rights (Fasterling & Demuijnck, 2013). In this way, HRDD introduces a more comprehensive and ethically grounded dimension to risk assessment, focusing on adverse human rights impacts.

Despite its increasing institutionalisation, the HRDD continues to be the subject of ongoing debate and criticism. In the following section, I will explain the main concerns that affect this form of due diligence. A key issue is whether HRDD should function as a stand-alone process or be integrated into a broader Enterprise Risk Management (ERM) framework. Some scholars argue that HRDD overlaps with existing due diligence tools, as suggested by the UNGPs, which adopt a preventive risk management perspective to address human rights issues (Schiller & Prpich, 2014). As a result, HRDD is often conceptualised as a form of internal control that addresses risks in the public interest. While HRDD and ERM share procedural similarities, such as assessing actual and potential impacts, integrating findings, tracking responses, and communicating, HRDD requires a dialogic and participatory approach that favours stakeholder engagement over probabilistic analysis.

A related problem is the widespread argument of the "business case for human rights", which suggests that the pursuit of corporate value and respect for human rights are compatible in the long term (Carroll & Shabana, 2010; Monciardini et al., 2021; Wettstein, 2021). However, such instrumental reasoning risks minimising the moral imperative of human rights, which can lead to superficial compliance and the neglect of structural social harms (Fasterling, 2017). Embedding HRDD in ERM frameworks, therefore, requires a genuine corporate commitment to human rights values. Without such a commitment, companies may be limited to providing minimal information aimed at meeting regulatory or reputational expectations rather than effecting substantive change (Fasterling, 2017).

Another challenge is the conceptualisation and measurement of human rights risk. Human rights risk, which is often confused with the broader concept of social risk, is more specifically defined as the "potential adverse human rights impact" of business activities (Bekefi et al., 2006). Social risk, on the other hand, refers to how public perception may affect corporate value. Treating human rights risk merely as a subset of social risk can obscure its normative underpinnings. Therefore, companies are called upon to develop empirically grounded tools that assess human rights risk on moral rather than purely economic grounds (Fasterling, 2017; McCorquodale & Nolan, 2021).

This normative focus is also relevant to the practice of social auditing within the HRDD process. According to the OECD Guidelines, social audits aim to verify companies' compliance with human rights standards (Ford & Nolan, 2020). However, traditional social audits are often based on superficial, checklist-based inspections conducted in a limited timeframe. To go beyond such "tick-the-box" exercises, social auditing needs to focus on continuous learning, prevention, and the protection of rights. This requires empowering workers, increasing the transparency of audit procedures, and improving access to redress mechanisms (Hess, 2021).

All these considerations, assuming that integrating HRDD into the ERM is sufficient to fulfil corporate human rights responsibilities are, therefore, misleading. HRDD is a complex multi-stakeholder process that goes beyond the boundaries of corporate governance (McCorquodale & Nolan, 2021). HRDD not only focuses on human rights abuses but also intersects with global environmental and sustainability frameworks, including the Paris Agreement, the OECD Guidelines for Multinational Enterprises, and ESG reporting standards (Shift, 2017; Buhmann et al., 2019; Buhmann, 2018). In this broader context, companies must also consider the potential human rights harms that may result from environmental initiatives, such as the transition to renewable energy or the adoption of regenerative agriculture. HRDD plays a central role in mitigating these risks, particularly in protecting vulnerable communities and ensuring access to remedies. Effective implementation requires sector-specific multi-stakeholder collaboration, including the active involvement of indigenous peoples, local communities, business partners, and suppliers (Areias, 2024).

Conversely, environmental degradation, including climate change, biodiversity loss, and water scarcity, poses a direct threat to the enjoyment of human rights. The increasing recognition of the interconnectedness of environmental and human rights concerns has led to human rights and environmental due diligence (HREDD) becoming a regulatory priority, particularly in the European Union (Dehbi & Martin-Ortega, 2023; Hess, 2021).

3.4 The Evolution Pathways of HRDD According to National and International Regulations

Over time, both national and international laws have recognised the role of actors other than states in the protection of human rights, including primarily businesses, especially those involved in international activities. However, to this day, few legal obligations require businesses to uphold human rights (Hess, 2021). Instead, many initiatives are carried out as a result of soft law standards, including the development of codes of conduct and the adoption of policies aimed at preventing human rights violations. These initiatives are often driven by public pressure and corporate awareness of their "moral responsibility" towards stakeholders. This limitation also extends to the positive obligation of due diligence, which, in the absence of binding regulations, remains one of the additional self-regulation mechanisms largely left to the discretion of businesses. Consequently, there is a pressing need for a process of legitimising corporate respect for human rights and a greater standardisation of due diligence practices (Nolan & Taylor, 2009).

This process began with Ruggie's report and the development of the UNGPs, and predominantly with the introduction of the OECD Guidelines for Multinational Companies. These guidelines represent a set of "principles and standards of conduct for a non-legal actor" (Bueno et al., 2024). The effects of both UNGP and OECD guidelines have been relevant for companies, particularly those operating in conflict-affected countries. In response to these requirements, companies have mainly focused on the adoption of policies and reporting, which are fundamental pillars of due diligence. At the European level, the 2014 directive (the EU 2014/95 Directive) previously required businesses to adopt a "report or explain" approach aimed at identifying, preventing, and mitigating observed risks, while reporting this information to stakeholders (Buhmann, 2018). Similarly, in 2006, the GRI standards introduced new guidelines for human rights reporting in line with UN principles. However, despite the adoption of these regulations, the corporate human rights reporting context remained weak (O'Brien & Dhanarajan, 2016). In recent years, the CSRD[1] and ESRS standards have brought about an important change by defining human rights through the concepts of "sustainability matters" and "impact materiality". Indeed, standards S1–S4 describe how companies should report on the impacts of their activities on different categories of stakeholders. In addition, the standards are based on the UNGP and OECD principles regarding the reporting of due diligence activities. However, one of the main differences between ESRS and these standards is the focus of the latter on the collection and distribution of information and less on the actual behaviour of the companies involved (Litwin & Savourey, 2025).

[1] The directive is designed to supersede the 2014 directive on social and environmental reporting by adopting a broader perspective and encompassing more sustainability-related themes (European Commission, 2024).

Despite significant progress over time, national legislation remains essential for imposing due diligence on businesses and providing clear, unambiguous guidelines that facilitate the integration of human rights respect with existing international regulations (Bueno et al., 2024). Some nations, primarily in Europe, including France, Germany, Norway, the Netherlands and Switzerland, have already undergone this process of legitimisation. The Duty of Vigilance Law, introduced in France in 2017, requires large businesses to implement due diligence procedures to identify and prevent human rights abuses. The Dutch Child Labour Due Diligence Law (2019), the National Action Plan for Business and Human Rights and the Due Diligence Guidelines in Norway (2015 and 2020), the German Supply Chain Act in 2021, and the Responsible Business Initiative in Switzerland (2018) came after it (Wettstein, 2022).

The CSDDD (EU Directive 2024/1760) is a significant development at the supranational level that aims to harmonise earlier national and European due diligence laws while addressing the need for certainty for businesses. The principal objective of the directive is to enable companies to "*identify and address adverse human rights and environmental impacts of their actions inside and outside Europe*" (European Commission, 2024). Its final objective is to create a structured framework for companies to reduce the impact of corporate activities on the environment and to reduce human rights violations caused by companies (Elbel et al., 2023). The directive arises from a lengthy negotiation process involving various parties, including NGOs, nations, businesses, and citizens. The European Commission justifies it as a tool to legislate a practice, namely due diligence, that many businesses already engage in voluntarily, concerning both environmental and social sustainability concerns (Thorens et al., 2025). In the context of human rights, this primarily pertains to the impacts arising from particular business activities, as outlined by various international instruments. The UNGPs, OECD guidelines, ILO Conventions, the EU Taxonomy, and the CSRD are the main elements that define the larger regulatory framework in which the directive is a part.

The directive targets large European companies with over 1000 employees and an annual turnover of €450 million, irrespective of their sector. The directive also applies to businesses outside the European context which have more than €450 million in turnover in a year in the European area. The directive not only involves companies' internal activities, but it also requires them to perform due diligence on their supply chains, which include upstream and downstream activities by other actors. Determining the degree of influence the business has and differentiating between impacts caused by the business alone, by the business and a subsidiary or partner, or by a third party alone makes this aspect extremely complex.

The primary innovation is the mandatory requirement that businesses conduct due diligence; in fact, failure to comply may result in penalties or the cessation of harmful operations. In order to ensure that the directive is properly implemented and that victims of violations have access to justice, each country has to establish a national authority (European Commission, 2025).Since its proposal in February 2022 and approval on July 25, 2024, the directive has been revolutionising how companies evaluate their environmental and human rights impacts in tandem with the CSRD. It also serves as one of the legislative instruments intended to accomplish the SDGs that the UN has advocated.

Many stakeholders appreciated the directive, but some have criticised it for being ambiguous and unclear about the desired results. Furthermore, one of the main risks is that it could become merely a "tick-the-box" exercise, primarily based on reporting and social auditing without altering the perspective businesses adopt when considering the human rights connected with their activities (Deva et al., 2023).

Implementing the directive outside of the European context is prompting third countries, such as Switzerland and South Korea, to adapt (Neri-Castracane et al., 2024). However, Bradford defines this phenomenon as the "de facto Brussels effect", alongside "de jure Brussels". This has been criticised as "neo-colonial in nature" and merely another form of the "Global North" imposing regulations on the "Global South" (Bueno et al., 2024; Thorens et al., 2025).

In 2025, the European Commission launched a new package of proposals aimed at simplifying sustainability reporting and due diligence rules to increase the competitiveness of European companies. Specifically, the "Omnibus Package" seeks to reduce the complexity of requirements for companies by reducing or eliminating obligations for small and medium-sized enterprises. In the context of the CSDDD, the measures are intended to simplify sustainability due diligence obligations to avoid unnecessary costs, reduce burdens and negative effects on small and medium-sized enterprises, increase the harmonisation of obligations within the European context, and eliminate EU civil liability conditions, while ensuring one of the cornerstones of the directive: the right of victims to compensation in the event of damage related to non-compliance with the directive. The evolution of HRDD legislation is represented in Table 3.1.

Finally, one of the main changes concerns timings, as the application of the rule for larger companies is expected to be postponed by 1 year, while the adoption of the guidelines is expected to be brought forward by 1 year (July 2026) (European Commission, 2025). The need for this intervention and the expected benefits are explained in the following message: "We are significantly simplifying compliance for large companies, while upholding the core objective of the CSDDD to prevent companies from indirectly contributing to exploitative business practices, harming human rights, the climate, or the environment through their value chains. We also ensure smaller business partners are not burdened by excessive information requests. By striking this balance, we hold companies accountable for their actions, and at the same time, we promote more transparent and responsible business operations globally". *Michael McGrath, Commissioner for Democracy, Justice, the Rule of Law, and Consumer Protection.*

Although the directive has faced criticism regarding its application, it marks a significant milestone in the history of BHR. Both academic and professional communities are curious to understand its impact on corporate behaviour and the broader implications for society.

In detail, Fig. 3.1 summarises the main changes introduced by the CSDDD for companies. The figure highlights four interconnected dimensions: governance and

Table 3.1 Main regulation instruments concerning HRDD

Year	Instrument	Key obligation	Level	Nature
2000/2011[a]	OECD Guidelines for Multinational Enterprises	Voluntary due diligence across value chains	International	Soft law
2006	GRI Standards—Human Rights Reporting	Disclose HR impacts in sustainability reports	International	Soft law
2011	UNGPs—Pillar II (HRDD as core obligation)	Identify, prevent, mitigate, and remedy HR impacts	International (UN)	Soft law
2014	EU NFRD (2014/95/EU) Non-Financial Reporting Dir.	Report or explain HR and environmental risks	European Union	Semi-binding
2017	French Duty of Vigilance	Mandatory HRDD for large French companies	National (France)	Binding
2019	Dutch Child Labour Due Diligence Law	Due diligence to prevent child labour in supply chains	National (NL)	Binding
2021	German Supply Chain Act	HR and environmental due diligence across supply chains	National (DE)	Binding
2022	CSRD + ESRS Standards	Disclose due diligence activities under ESRS S1–S4 standards	European Union	Binding
2024	CSDDD (EU 2024/1760)	Mandatory HRDD for firms >1000 employees/€450M turnover	European Union	Binding
2025	EU Omnibus Package Simplification of CSDDD and CSRD	Reduce burdens, exempt SMEs, Postpone CSDDD by 1 year	European Union	Binding

Source: Author's own elaboration
[a]The OECD Guidelines were originally adopted in 2000 and substantially revised in 2011 to include a dedicated human rights chapter aligned with the UNGPs

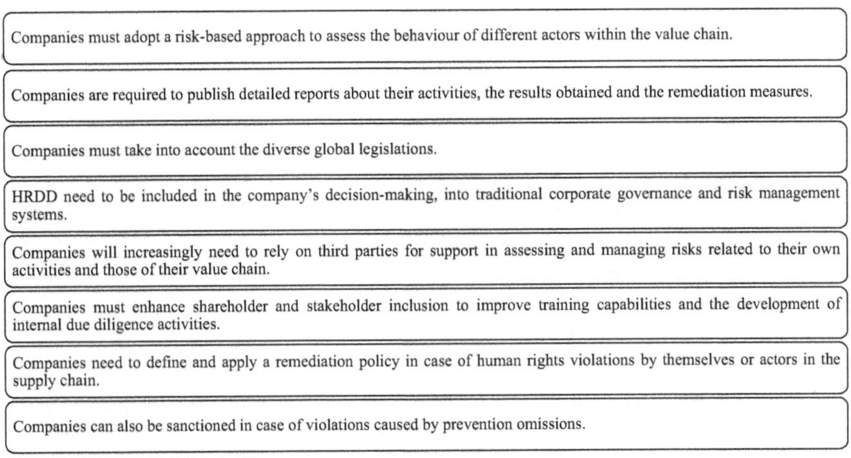

Source: author's own elaboration

Fig. 3.1 Changes after the CSDDD introduction. *Source*: Author's own elaboration

accountability, requiring companies to integrate HRDD into internal structures and board-level oversight; supply chain management and stakeholder engagement.

These dimensions illustrate the comprehensive nature of the Directive and the organisational adjustments required for companies.

3.5 Institutional Pressures and HRDD

The integration of human rights considerations into corporate decision-making is often perceived as a balancing act between governmental regulations and sectoral self-regulation, frequently implemented through CSR initiatives. The adherence to human rights principles is further driven by the increasing expectations of various stakeholders, including institutional investors, shareholders, and other key actors (Flynn, 2020; Litwin & Savourey, 2025). Failure to comply with human rights standards can result in significant reputational damage for companies, with potential legal ramifications that may cost millions in litigation and defence expenses. Therefore, beyond binding regulations, companies must adopt voluntary initiatives to mitigate costs and avoid prolonged legal disputes. Among these initiatives, corporate governance mechanisms, such as internal control systems and external auditing, play a crucial role in promoting voluntary compliance and the privatisation of legal frameworks (McCorquodale & Neely, 2022).

Given the pressures exerted by governments and stakeholders, the adoption of HRDD requires companies to acknowledge the potential impact of their activities on human rights and to account for the associated consequences (Hess, 2021; Graetz & Franks, 2013). The implementation of the new directive, albeit with certain adjustments from its initial proposals, marks a paradigm shift not only for European companies but also for global markets. While previous directives and national regulations had already mandated due diligence practices in environmental and social matters, these requirements were largely discretionary, leading to limited engagement from companies (Lopatta et al., 2023). In contrast, the new directive imposes an obligation on large corporations to conduct and report on due diligence activities according to a unified European framework. This development can be examined through the lens of institutional theory, which posits that companies must align with the dominant institutions in their environment to achieve social legitimacy (DiMaggio & Powell, 1983; Dowling & Pfeffer, 1975).

According to this theory, companies are not just economic actors, but also political entities that, alongside states, contribute to the provision of public goods and services. Institutions can be formal, such as political, legal, and economic frameworks, or informal, encompassing cultural norms, behavioural codes, and professional standards (Favotto & Kollman, 2022). A core concept of this theory is institutional isomorphism, which manifests in three forms: mimetic, coercive, and normative (DiMaggio & Powell, 1983; Meyer & Rowan, 1977). Institutional theory is often used to analyse how companies behave socially in response to internal and external pressures, and it is useful for explaining the shift from voluntary to mandatory corporate reporting (Zampella et al., 2025). Rather than dictating how firms will respond to or reject institutional expectations, it illustrates how companies seek social legitimacy through competitive pressures, regulatory compliance, and industry-wide best practices. In the vein of HRDD, the dual perspective of "do no harm" and "do more good" is one instrument through which companies can enhance their legitimacy and create value for themselves and society (Buhmann et al., 2019).

In the HRDD context, coercive pressures necessitate firms to adopt due diligence practices to maintain legitimacy by ensuring compliance with legal norms, social expectations, and contextual values. It is exemplified by human rights agreements, for example, national and international laws, as the recent development of the CSDDD and the stringency of the "rule of law" that governments apply to national actors (Giuliani et al., 2023). Normative pressures stem from the proliferation of industry standards advocating for mandatory due diligence (Flynn & Walker, 2021). These pressures are "meta-norms" influencing company behaviour and establishing international benchmarks for human rights practices as seen in UN or OECD initiatives (Giuliani et al., 2023). Finally, mimetic pressures compel firms to adopt these practices to secure reputational advantages and align with industry best practices, thereby responding to stakeholder expectations (Buhmann, 2018; Christ et al., 2019). However, according to neo-institutional theory, firms often react to normative and isomorphic pressures by adopting symbolic measures of legitimacy, such as codes of conduct, industry standards, and stakeholder engagement, that do not necessarily translate into substantive behavioural changes. These are merely superficial or "ceremonial" forms of conformity with institutional pressure (Meyer & Rowan, 1977). Consequently, the likelihood of avoidance and defiance strategies remains high (Rogerson et al., 2024). This dynamic underscores the need for a thorough evaluation of the CSDDD's role in promoting more action-oriented disclosure while acknowledging the associated costs and risks. The institutional pressures are particularly pronounced for multinational corporations, which have been historically designated as actors responsible for human rights violations. They constitute most companies addressed by the CSDDD and have considerable influence in the international arena by driving isomorphic pressures within their sectors. However, they are also subjected to substantial internal and external pressures, both in their home countries and in host markets (Kostova & Zaheer, 1999; Kostova et al., 2008). Multinational corporations tend to be more pressured by international standards in addition to local regulations, and by the scrutiny from international institutions, NGOs, and activists (Colovic et al., 2019). In the human rights context, their role is particularly relevant since HRDD adoption remains largely confined to multinational firms, while their supply chain actors often remain obscured from scrutiny. This opacity prevents full compliance and allows human rights violations within supply chains to go unnoticed. The CSDDD aims to address this issue by ensuring greater transparency across the value chain, even for entities operating outside the EU.

3.6 The Impact of CSDDD

After the introduction of the CSDDD, the behaviour of companies will be modified in response to institutional forces. As a binding regulation, the directive will exert significant pressure on companies to ensure compliance. In addition, one of the most relevant novelties is the requirement for Member States to designate supervisory authorities responsible for monitoring compliance and imposing sanctions for non-compliance. Consequently, companies should necessarily comply with the directive to avoid costly legal proceedings and potential reputational damage.

Despite the application to the entire European context, corporate responses are likely to vary depending on the country of origin. Addressed countries should translate the directive into national laws, and while some European countries have already implemented mandatory HRDD regulations, others are introducing such frameworks for the first time. Consequently, we expect a different level of maturity in the adoption of HRDD practices according to the country of origin. Indeed, although institutional theory is often associated with isomorphism, it also provides a useful lens for understanding behavioural heterogeneity among firms (Christ et al., 2019; Flynn & Walker, 2021).

In addition to the country heterogeneity, companies will respond to the directive differently based on factors such as size and sector. In this sense, the prominence of human rights within industry norms will be a key determinant of corporate behaviour. Sectoral variation will remain a primary source of heterogeneity, as the relevance and salience of human rights issues differ significantly across industries. For instance, firms in manufacturing, fashion, wholesale, and retail have already made substantial adjustments in response to stakeholder pressures, whereas companies in lower-risk sectors may not have adopted comparable practices. Moreover, firms in high-risk sectors, where the potential for human rights violations is more pronounced, often allocate greater financial resources to risk prevention and insurance. These firms are expected to be more prepared to meet the requirements of the CSDDD (Flynn, 2020). Finally, mimetic isomorphism is expected to play a role, as firms tend to emulate perceived industry leaders. This dynamic may lead to improvements in due diligence practices even among firms not directly subject to the directive or those facing delayed implementation, as they seek reputational benefits by aligning with emerging standards.

In light of the described context, the introduction of the CSDDD will bring both benefits and challenges for companies, particularly concerning HRDD. On the positive side, the directive will help create a clearer and more consistent framework for managing human rights risks, reducing regulatory uncertainty, and protecting businesses from potential legal disputes and reputational damage. External pressure will push companies to improve their practices, not only to comply with the new obligations but also to gain a competitive advantage by following the example of industry leaders. Institutional investors and rating agencies value companies' commitment to human rights due diligence, and better evaluation could lead to financial benefits such as reduced risk and increased financial performance (Buhmann, 2023).

Moreover, companies with good due diligence practices, especially if embedded in the corporate culture, will benefit from the support of their stakeholders. Furthermore, increased transparency and stakeholder engagement will strengthen trust in the market, helping to make HRDD a more established and widely adopted practice in their sector. Companies with structured HRDD frameworks that are action-oriented rather than merely disclosure-oriented could have a better ability to attract and retain consumers, partners, and gain a competitive advantage (McCorquodale et al., 2017; Principale, 2023). Adopting such practices proactively rather than solely based on compliance would greatly influence industry behaviour, influence public opinion, and enable better performance compared to competitors.

However, adapting to the CSDDD will also present some challenges, mainly related to the companies' lack of readiness to adopt the directive and the associated costs. Costs can mainly be divided into operational costs related to routine due diligence activities and ongoing maintenance, and transaction costs related to expenses and investments needed to modify internal activities and those related to the value chain. Companies will need to allocate resources to map and monitor their entire value chain, a particularly burdensome task for smaller firms or those with complex global supply chains. Other challenges include the potential disadvantages that European businesses could face compared to competitors that fall outside the scope of the directive. This limitation could be addressed through subsidies and state incentives or by leveraging digitalisation. Additionally, foreign businesses entering contracts with European companies may feel the impact and reconsider their relationships. One solution could be the implementation of shared responsibility, which aims for a win-win approach rather than a win-lose scenario based on a zero-sum game of responsibilities among the various actors involved in the relationships (Leite et al., 2024).

For non-European actors, non-compliance can cause legal punishments, such as exclusion from the European market. On the contrary, the increased rigidity concerning the value chain entails a reassessment of pre-existing business relationships, with the risk of having to change long-established partners and being exposed to the risks and costs associated with this change.

The adoption of HRDD practices in a superficial manner, that is, based on concealment (Oliver, 1991) or "cosmetic compliance" (Hess, 2021), leads to reputational damage. One of the main consequences of these misbehaviours is boycotts, resulting in reduced profitability and increasing pressure from public bodies and other stakeholders such as consumers, investors, media, and especially NGOs. The risk of a simple "tick-the-box" exercise is very high, especially if companies do not include HRDD in their culture and business model. This risk is particularly high considering the high rate of standardisation required by the directive, which does not impose differences in its adoption except at the dimension level. Hence, there is a fear that the one-size-fits-all approach will generate imitative behaviour based solely on the need for compliance and reduce the effectiveness of the directive per se. This is particularly true for non-European companies or companies with fewer financial resources, which therefore will suffer from increased costs that are not necessarily aligned with better HRDD results. The ultimate consequence is to potentially slow down change rather than accelerate its implementation.

Similarly, another challenge that companies and institutions need to manage is the uncertainty of institutional standards. The directive has undergone several modifications since its initial draft, reflecting the ongoing debates and differing perspectives within the international community regarding the extent and nature of corporate due diligence obligations. The ongoing revisions and disputed requirements foster an environment of regulatory uncertainty. The situation becomes more complex when considering the already fragmented framework of human rights law at the international level (Litwin & Savourey, 2025). This may lead some companies to adopt concealment strategies, ultimately resulting in symbolic compliance. This form of adherence allows firms to give the impression of compliance while continuing their usual operations, which may still present risks to human rights and the environment (Rogerson et al., 2024).

In addition, the risk of decoupling is high when the conformity with international rules is not aligned with efficiency or stakeholder expectations, or they are inconsistent (Buhmann, 2018; Meyer & Rowan, 1977). Given the complexity of global supply chains and the difficulties in monitoring corporate practices beyond direct operations, enforcement mechanisms may struggle to identify cases of noncompliance, especially when companies strategically withhold or manipulate information. The effectiveness of punitive actions depends on the ability of regulatory bodies to conduct thorough investigations, establish clear accountability, and impose sanctions that serve as credible deterrents. However, given the diverse regulatory landscapes across jurisdictions, harmonising enforcement efforts remains a significant challenge, potentially weakening the directive's overall impact (Roszkowska-Menkes et al., 2024).

A potential solution to the above-mentioned limitations is stressed in the directive itself, and it is represented by stakeholder engagement and the evaluation of their interests in due diligence execution. Stakeholders are a link between the negative obligation of companies to do no harm and the positive obligation to contribute to society. In light of the UNGP, the SDGs, and the CSDDD, stakeholder consultation is an important pillar for recognising potential violations and finding effective solutions. By engaging with stakeholders, companies can facilitate the management of current and potential impacts and contribute to social and local needs. Consequently, there is a need to extend due diligence processes beyond the corporate context to ensure a "social licence to operate" and create further value for the company and society (Buhmann et al., 2019). Consequently, the application of the CSDDD requires companies to no longer limit themselves to a formal and superficial approach to stakeholder consultation, but to develop structured and continuous mechanisms of dialogue with stakeholders, including workers, local communities, NGOs, and responsible investors. More specifically, the more vulnerable parts need to be included in the decision-making processes (Elbel et al., 2023). This implies the need to build relationships based on transparency, mutual trust, and recognition of the active role of stakeholders in defining corporate strategies (Avant et al., 2023; Olsen et al., 2025).

However, one of the main risks related to the expansion of stakeholder engagement is greenwashing or social washing, that is, the possibility that companies implement engagement practices only in a symbolic way, without really integrating stakeholder demands into decision-making processes. Moreover, ineffective interaction can increase the risk of reputational conflicts, especially if stakeholders perceive that their concerns are not adequately taken into account. To avoid such critical issues, CSDDD requires a profound cultural change within companies that goes beyond mere regulatory compliance. This risk requires a broader range of stakeholders (such as auditors, data providers, ESG rating agencies, and investors) to become more familiar with assessing the actual differences between the disclosure and respect for human rights and the actual implementation of the Directive. In addition, internal stakeholders such as employees and board members need to be involved in training and learning paths in order to correctly implement the various requirements that are part of the new regulatory infrastructure (CSDDD, CSRD, and ESRS). Finally, from the investors' perspective, they need to include human rights assessments in their investment decisions and use their voting rights as leverage to demand human rights strategies and good due diligence practices (Litwin & Savourey, 2025).

For HRDD to become a tool for radical transformation, companies must redefine their values and internal culture, incorporating sustainability and human rights principles into strategic decisions. This means moving from a reactive and defensive approach to a proactive model, where respect for human rights is perceived not as a constraint, but as an opportunity to contribute to the defence of vulnerable parts and ultimately contribute to long-term value. This change requires investment in training, development of new managerial skills, and review of incentive systems, so that due diligence is not just a formal requirement, but a lever for innovation and competitive advantage (Buhmann, 2017).

Despite the necessity to introduce a unique framework for the application of HRDD, some doubts remain because it might not be enough to ensure the resolution of human rights violations without a profound intervention to reconceptualise how companies think and operate (Choudhury, 2023; Deva et al., 2023). The directive builds on the business case for respecting human rights, which suggests that integrating human rights considerations into corporate strategy is not only an ethical imperative but also beneficial for long-term value creation, reducing risks and enhancing reputation (Carroll & Shabana, 2010; Monciardini et al., 2021; Wettstein, 2021). However, as the directive is still being revised, its impact remains uncertain. In the coming years, we will be able to assess whether it effectively supports this alignment between business success and human rights or if concealment strategies and cosmetic compliance characterise corporate responses. The proposed framework concerning the implementation of the CSDDD on the behaviour of companies, under the lens of the institutional theory, is presented in Table 3.2. The upper section identifies the institutional forces driving corporate behaviour, highlighting the heterogeneity of responses according to the country of origin, sector, and size. The middle section maps potential benefits and challenges associated with the CSDDD, while the lower section proposes potential solutions, such as stakeholder

Table 3.2 Conceptual framework

Component	Explanation
Institutional components	
Institutional Forces and Compliance Pressure	CSDDD introduces binding regulations for companies to conduct HR and environmental due diligence. Companies need to adapt to avoid litigation and reputational harm (Christ et al., 2019; Flynn & Walker, 2021).
National and industry heterogeneity	Countries with existing HRDD laws (e.g. France and Germany) are more advanced than those introducing them. Differences in national institutional maturity will lead to varying degrees of compliance. Company characteristics such as size and sector further influence responses. High-risk sectors (e.g. manufacturing, fashion) are generally more advanced in HRDD implementation (Flynn, 2020). Mimetic isomorphism may push others to emulate industry leaders, even if not directly obligated.
Pro and cons	
Benefits of the CSDDD	Offers regulatory clarity, reduces uncertainty, and may enhance reputational capital. Institutional investors and ESG rating agencies reward firms with strong HRDD frameworks (Buhmann, 2023). Proactive, embedded HRDD approaches can build a competitive advantage (McCorquodale et al., 2017; Principale, 2023). Companies that go beyond formal compliance may gain stakeholder trust and loyalty.
Challenges and risks	High operational and transaction costs for mapping and monitoring complex global supply chains. Risk of "Tick-the-box" exercise (Oliver, 1991) or superficial adaptation (Hess, 2021). Regulatory uncertainty due to ongoing revisions (Rogerson et al., 2024). Enforcement challenges due to fragmented jurisdictional contexts (Buhmann, 2018; Meyer & Rowan, 1977).
Potential solutions	
Stakeholder engagement	Stakeholders link the company's "do no harm" obligations to positive social contributions. CSDDD encourages meaningful dialogue with workers, NGOs, communities, and investors (Buhmann et al., 2019). Genuine stakeholder integration can strengthen a company's social license to operate. But risks of social/greenwashing remain if engagement is only symbolic.
Toward Strategic Transformation	HRDD should drive cultural and strategic shifts, not just legal compliance. Requires investment in training, new skills, and revised incentives (Buhmann, 2017). Long-term success involves embedding HRDD into corporate values and business models. Yet, doubts persist about whether regulation alone can change business behaviour (Choudhury, 2023; Deva et al., 2023).

Source: Author's own elaboration

engagement and strategic transformation as main mechanisms through which companies can move beyond formal compliance to substantive HRDD adoption.

3.7 Conclusions

The present chapter proposes a theoretical framework that emphasises the characteristics of HRDD from an economic and managerial standpoint, adopting a purely corporate perspective. In order to identify corporate behaviour patterns, it is necessary to observe the institutional context of reference, characterised by the transition from a regulatory framework oriented towards soft law instruments to increasingly binding instruments, first at the national level and then at the regional level through the introduction of the CSDDD. This directive, which signifies a departure from previous interventions, constitutes an evolution that is congruent with the prevailing logic of institutional pressures. Consequently, the focus of the chapter is to highlight the potential impact of the directive on corporate behaviour through the lens of institutional theory. The theoretical framework presented illustrates the advantages of the directive in filling gaps in legitimacy and accountability and highlights the potential benefits for businesses and institutions. However, it also points out possible side effects, such as reputational damage and the risk of cosmetic compliance. The paper presents some solutions, such as consultation with interested parties and the inclusion of stakeholders, and the introduction of the issue of human rights defence into corporate culture and strategy.

In consideration of the framework that has been delineated, and given the pertinence of the subject matter, it is evident that the framework offers significant contributions, both from a theoretical standpoint and from a practical perspective. From a theoretical point of view, the contribution offers the following implications. Firstly, this is one of the first theoretical works to analyse the advantages and disadvantages of CSDDD, highlighting the contrast between principle and practice. Secondly, the study contributes to extant literature by highlighting how companies will react to institutional pressures introduced by new regulatory requirements, emphasising the pros and cons of such intervention. The present study contributes to the broadening of the application of institutional theory. Although this theory has been extensively utilised in the domain of sustainability and non-financial reporting, its application in this particular context enables the identification of both forms of isomorphism and differences in behaviour based on divergent pressures (Brammer et al., 2012). Moreover, concerning this theory, one of the primary risks associated with the implementation of the CSDDD is emphasised: namely, that of a "tick-the-box" exercise with the contrary effect to that desired. The conceptual framework developed in this chapter directly guides the empirical analysis of Chap. 4. The identification of coercive, mimetic, and normative pressures as drivers of HRDD adoption provides the theoretical basis for the selection of the independent variables tested in the regression models. The discussion of legitimacy theory and its relationship with institutional theory influences the formulation of the hypotheses concerning media exposure, stakeholder engagement, and past human rights violations. In addition, the framework's emphasis on the heterogeneity of corporate responses, shaped by country of origin, sector, and size, informs the design of the quantitative analysis, which compares European and non-European companies before and after the introduction of the CSDDD.

The work also offers useful implications for various stakeholders. The objective of the present study is to emphasise the potential repercussions of the novel regulatory intervention on corporate conduct. It is incumbent upon companies to consider the necessity of modifying their internal structures to comply with the regulations or to adopt proactive measures. The necessary changes primarily concern the reformulation of internal governance, supply chain management, and an assessment of the costs and opportunities associated with these changes. The assessments presented have considerable utility for civil society, given that the European regulatory framework acknowledges the expanding role of communities in safeguarding human rights and in facilitating the definition and monitoring of due diligence processes. Moreover, as has been documented, multi-stakeholder initiatives are recognised as pivotal instruments for ensuring the representation of the voices of workers, NGOs, and local communities in the decision-making processes of corporations.

It is ultimately posited that the most substantial contribution of this study is directed towards policymakers. Local and national governments are obliged to consider the substantial alterations introduced by the CSDDD and to refrain from regulatory fragmentation, thus facilitating coordination with national and international instruments. Legislators must consider the costs and disadvantages that will inevitably be caused by the directive, especially for the most vulnerable parties. It is their responsibility to define policies and instruments to avoid excessive damage to competitiveness. In conclusion, these bodies must establish effective control and enforcement systems that minimise the risk of symbolic compliance.

The challenge posed by the CSDDD is twofold: firstly, to adapt to a new regulatory framework, and secondly, to demonstrate that HRDD can evolve into a practice that can have a real impact on people's lives. It is within this balance between promise and implementation that the future of the relationship between business and human rights will be maintained.

Chapter 4
Examining Corporate Readiness for the CSDDD: An Empirical Test of Institutional and Legitimacy Pressures

4.1 Introduction

In recent years, companies have been confronted with several challenges in the context in which they operate, including environmental, social, and governance issues (Ioannou & Serafeim, 2012). On the social front, the global supply chain has repeatedly come under scrutiny from non-governmental organisations and international institutions due to human rights violations resulting from the exploitation of workers or the degradation of environmental conditions in exploited areas and local communities (Cahaya & Hervina, 2019; Islam & McPhail, 2011; Jabotinsky & Sarel, 2025; Smith et al., 2024). In addition, the more companies operate outside their national environment, the more they are exposed to pressure from various stakeholders, including regulators, investors, consumers, and civil society (Narula, 2019). To reduce the risk of such violations and alleviate pressure from these stakeholders, companies must apply the HRDD introduced by the United Nations and the OECD (Leite et al., 2024). Consequently, the governance of human rights has evolved into a framework that combines both voluntary and mandatory standards for businesses (Reiner et al., 2025). Key elements of this framework include the UNGPs, the OECD Guidelines for Multinational Enterprises, and various non-financial reporting standards such as the GRI (Burritt & Christ, 2023; McPhail & Ferguson, 2016; Preuss & Brown, 2012). These standards have encouraged companies to disclose information on human rights, human rights abuses, and the practices used by companies to mitigate the associated risks (Litwin & Savourey, 2025). At the same time, several countries, including France, Germany, the Netherlands, Switzerland, and the United Kingdom, have adopted national regulations requiring companies to implement and report on HRDD. However, despite these measures, the regulatory framework remains quite fragmented and inconsistent; these regulations are mostly limited in scope, apply only to certain companies or sectors, and are generally non-binding (Maluțan et al., 2024). This means that HRDD is not applied

I. Mastrorocco, *From Voluntary Responsibility to Regulatory Compliance*, SIDREA Series in Accounting and Business Administration,
https://doi.org/10.1007/978-3-032-34492-2_4

uniformly and, above all, not in a substantive manner and often serves more as an element of social washing than as a tool to mitigate the risks of human rights violations (Rogerson et al., 2024). The introduction of the CSDDD, therefore, marks a break with the past and represents the first binding and standardised legislative measure for Europe and also outside the continent (Principale, 2023). The directive aims to recognise, prevent, and mitigate human rights and environmental risks along the global value chain. Although the directive will not be fully implemented until 2027 through integration into the regulations of individual countries, it is already having an impact on both the academic debate on BHR and on companies.

Despite the relevance of the topic of HRDD and the introduction of CSDDD with the associated considerations, some research gaps remain about this topic. In particular, few studies to date analyse the expected impact of the Directive, and the existing studies mainly follow a theoretical approach that examines the potential advantages and disadvantages without assessing the behaviour and reaction of companies to these new regulatory interventions (Leite et al., 2024). Moreover, the existing studies tend to focus on compliance mechanisms without assessing how the combination of regulatory pressure and legitimacy dynamics may influence firms' behaviour. To address these research gaps, the study proposes an integrated framework that empirically tests and extends the model presented in the third chapter by combining institutional theory and legitimacy theory. The aim of the study is formulated in the following research question:

RQ: How does the adoption of the CSDDD affect the adoption of human rights due diligence, and how do companies reconcile institutional compliance and legitimacy concerns?

This study makes three main contributions to the existing literature. First, given the lack of quantitative studies on this topic identified in the second chapter the study applies various quantitative methods, including difference-in-difference analysis, event study, and panel regression analysis, based on a sample of companies from the S&P 1200, to investigate whether and to what extent the CSDDD affects firms' behaviour in terms of HRDD practices, even in the early stages. The quantitative approach permits an evaluation of a large sample of companies to identify common patterns. Second, the study identifies several factors attributable to both institutional and legitimacy theory that influence HRDD practices, including international exposure, industry standards, media exposure, and, finally, past human rights abuses. The study is one of the first to examine the anticipatory impact of the CSDDD on HRDD in a global context, comparing companies that are and are not involved in the Directive. Third, by integrating two theoretical frameworks and robust quantitative analyses, the study contributes to the debate on BHR and HRDD and adds to the public debate by providing up-to-date evidence in line with the new legal framework. It also answers to the call of future research presented in the second chapter concerning the necessity to empirically evaluate the influence of the CSDDD implementation and the evaluation of the balance between institutional and legitimacy factors (cf. Chap. 2).

The rest of the chapter is organised as follows. Section 4.2 provides an overview of previous contributions to this topic, while Sect. 4.3 presents the two selected theoretical frameworks and research hypotheses. Section 4.4 describes the methodology used, and Sect. 4.5 presents the results obtained. Finally, Sect. 4.6 presents the discussions and Sect. 4.7 the conclusions with the theoretical and practical implications and limitations of the study.

4.2 Literature Review

In recent years, several corporate governance frameworks have gradually shifted from a purely financial perspective to one that includes management and reporting on environmental and social issues (García-Sánchez et al., 2025). Within this perspective, HRDD can be positioned both as a corporate governance paradigm comparable to more traditional systems such as internal control frameworks or ERM, and as a unique system in itself. The features that characterise HRDD have been outlined by Sherman (2022) and primarily relate to its focus compared to more conventional approaches. In particular, HRDD is centred on the rights holders rather than the economic interests of the company. In this respect, HRDD serves as a bridge in the ongoing debate between shareholder primacy and stakeholder orientation. In addition, HRDD is adopted by companies to minimise the risk of reputational damage or economic sanctions from stakeholders. It can, therefore, be seen as a risk management tool. The introduction of HRDD or the integration of reporting into management processes also creates learning opportunities for companies to reduce not only the risks to society but also the risks to themselves resulting from social sanctions (Buhmann, 2018). In line with previous assumptions and according to the UNGPs, HRDD "goes beyond simply identifying and managing material risks to the company itself" and includes the identification and mitigation of "risks to right-holders" (McPhail & Ferguson, 2025). This dual role is also recognised by financial markets and is evidenced by the inclusion of environmental and social factors in investment decisions (ESG investing), the significant reputational damage to which companies are exposed as a result of human rights abuses, and the inclusion of HRDD elements in common law systems, civil law jurisdictions, and trade regulations (Sherman, 2022). In this context, a shift from voluntary to mandatory HRDD (mHRDD) is defined as "the most effective means for the government to enshrine enhanced due diligence in law but backed by MNC responsibility and remedies for failure to achieve it" (Hess, 2021). Without mandatory rules, such as those already introduced in France and Germany or more recently in Europe with the CSDDD, it is difficult to foresee a genuine corporate commitment to improving human rights accountability and a good level of homogeneity in its implementation. However, as Chen and Sheehy (2025) argue, unless this liability extends to the board, it is unlikely to receive sufficient attention to effect meaningful change in day-to-day corporate behaviour, and the risk of mere "ticking off" is particularly high. In this respect, the CSDDD represents the first binding European regulation on HRDD that imposes explicit administrative oversight and civil liability obligations on boards. Since the directive was only recently approved, the process of familiarisation with the CSDDD is a crucial element to investigate (Kiewisch, 2025). Edelman (2016) has defined it as fundamental to transforming what is initially perceived as a vague law into effective operational practices. From the interviews conducted in the chocolate sector by Kiewisch (2025), it appears that companies not only expressed early support for mandatory due diligence but also initiated multi-stakeholder coordination initiatives. Nevertheless, the extent of adoption of the material practices strongly depends on the robustness of internal governance processes and the value chain context. Similarly, a survey by Jabotinsky and Sarel (2025) shows that while there is broad support for the governance mechanism of the CSDDD among managers and practitioners, there are concerns about the appropriateness of possible changes to the text and, above all, a lower perceived urgency for climate-related issues (see Omnibus Guideline, p. 8).

The emergence of the CSDDD as the first binding European regulation on human rights issues provides an ideal context to combine the findings from studies on the determinants of human rights policy adoption with those examining the causes of human rights violations. The adoption of human rights policies remains a controversial issue. Some scholars argue that policies alone are insufficient to reduce violations (Olsen et al., 2022; Nieri et al., 2023). On the other hand, Romito et al. (2025) find that the adoption of policies can have a positive impact on respect for human rights, as evidenced by a decrease in human rights violations as a result of cultural change and the implementation of new practices required by these policies. Studies by Ciravegna and Nieri (2022) and Giuliani et al. (2023) have shown that human rights violations are influenced by a combination of institutional factors, such as the institutional environment of the home country and the degree of internationalisation, as well as company-level variables, including financial performance, size, age, and ownership structure. In parallel, Wang et al. (2024) contribute to this debate by focusing on the determinants of human rights violations in global supply chains, in particular the role of "smart disclosure" in improving supplier visibility. Building on institutional theory, they conceptualise multinational corporations (MNCs) as institutional bearers whose ability to pass on desired norms is limited when potential users, such as suppliers, are not readily identifiable. Smart disclosure, by increasing visibility in global supply chains, can create pressure for compliance with standards, incentivise and support suppliers in a targeted manner, and thus reduce human rights violations.

Despite the present studies aiming at identifying determinant factors of human rights violations, as Cosa (2025) notes, there remains a gap in the comparative quantitative literature: Few studies have examined the effects of a binding regulatory regime from a longitudinal and cross-national perspective, simultaneously incorporating coercive, normative, mimetic, and legitimacy determinants. Cosa (2025), in line with Muchlinski's (2012) categorisation of corporate human rights obligations into three main types, legal, voluntary, and reputational, finds that such obligations can improve human rights performance, particularly through the role of grievance mechanisms and stakeholder engagement. Nevertheless, the author recognises that this relationship is shaped by geographic and sector-specific factors, as well as corporate governance characteristics. These considerations are closely related to the growing literature analysing how such commitments are communicated externally through disclosure practices. In this context, Christ et al. (2022) analyse the quantity and quality of modern slavery disclosure and conclude that the information provided is generally of low quality and predominantly narrative and descriptive. Such reporting is only marginally responsive to mimetic and normative pressures, and its limited information value indicates a potential disconnect between perceived and actual corporate behaviour.

From a broader perspective, McPhail and Ferguson (2025) trace the evolution of social and environmental accounting towards frameworks that incorporate human rights standards, such as GRI, IR, and ISSB. While IR and ISSB focus primarily on the interests and information needs of financial investors, GRI takes a broader stakeholder-centred approach. In line with the UNGPs, human rights reporting, especially when embedded in the HRDD, includes a "double materiality" perspective that goes beyond material risks to the company to include the identification and mitigation of risks to rights holders. BHR reporting differs from traditional social and environmental accounting because it places the concept of rights at the centre. Recent developments include external disclosure requirements under modern slavery legislation (e.g. in California and the UK), the French Duty of Vigilance Act of 2017, and the German Supply Chain Due Diligence Act of 2021, as well as the EU NFRD of 2014, the CSRD, and the CSDDD. Voluntary initiatives have also emerged, such as the Corporate Human Rights Benchmark (CHRB) in 2013, which, however, provides limited insight into actual human rights performance, and the Human Rights Reporting and Assurance Frameworks Initiative (RAFI) in 2015. Despite this progress, it is too early to determine whether these initiatives will lead to greater respect for human rights, and further research is needed to assess the extent to which human rights reporting contributes to corporate value, given the inherent difficulties in measuring human rights outcomes. Building on this literature, the following section develops the theoretical framework that guides the empirical analysis, drawing on institutional theory and legitimacy theory to identify the key pressures that shape corporate HRDD adoption.

4.3 Theoretical Framework and Hypotheses Development

Building on the conceptual framework developed in Chap. 3, the theoretical background developed in this chapter draws on two complementary perspectives: institutional theory and legitimacy theory. Although these theories are often applied separately in the literature, Chen and Roberts (2010) demonstrate that they share a common ontological foundation since both are system-oriented theories that view organisations as social entities embedded in a broader environment, and both explain organisational behaviour as shaped by external pressures rather than purely internal strategic calculations. Their levels of analysis, however, differ. Legitimacy theory operates at the broadest level, focusing on whether the value system of an organisation is congruent with the value system of society as a whole, and on the conditions under which organisations obtain or lose social acceptance (Suchman, 1995). Institutional theory, by contrast, operates at a more specific level, focusing on the patterns of established institutions as the symbolic representation of social values, and proposing that conformity to these institutionalised norms is the primary pathway through which organisations achieve legitimacy (DiMaggio & Powell, 1983; Chen & Roberts, 2010). The integration of these two frameworks is appropriate in the context of HRDD adoption, where companies simultaneously face field-level pressures to conform to emerging regulatory and industry standards and organisation-specific pressures to manage their reputational standing and restore social acceptance following human rights requirements. Together, the two theories provide a more complete explanatory model than either could offer alone.

According to the model developed by DiMaggio and Powell (1983), firms operate in an environment characterised by a strong process of homogenisation (isomorphism), which leads them to adopt similar structures and practices in response to different pressures from the institutional context. These pressures, which may be coercive, mimetic, or normative in nature, help to explain why organisations adopt HRDD practices not only for internal reasons, but also in response to external demands.

Coercive pressures stem from regulations and international agreements that impose minimum human rights standards on companies, the CSDDD being the most prominent recent example in the European context. In addition, the rigour of the rule of law in different countries plays a crucial role: where governments have robust legal systems and are more likely to sanction violations, companies tend to avoid opportunistic or harmful behaviour in relation to human rights (Giuliani et al., 2023).

In addition to this regulatory pressure, there is a mimetic pressure that occurs in contexts of uncertainty, leading companies to imitate the practices of actors perceived to be leading or performing best. Such imitation may result from observing the strategies of direct competitors, industry standards, or initiatives of external stakeholders, such as NGOs or international organisations, that set benchmarks and promote sectoral cooperation. Through this process, companies seek to mitigate reputational risks and signal their alignment with common best practices (Flynn & Walker, 2021; Giuliani et al., 2023). Finally, regulatory pressure arises from the role of professional organisations, trade associations, and international bodies that set standards of conduct and guidelines. These arise from a kind of "cultural" legitimisation that encourages companies to adhere to internationally shared meta-standards and principles, such as those established by the United Nations or the OECD. Such initiatives are not always binding, but they serve as a frame of reference that guides corporate behaviour and promotes convergence towards common practices to protect human rights (Flynn & Walker, 2021; Giuliani et al., 2023).

The introduction of CSDDD in 2024 represents one of the most significant regulatory changes in the area of corporate sustainability and human rights. From an institutional perspective, such binding rules create strong pressure for companies to comply, as they face significant risks and penalties for non-compliance. However, it is important to understand how this directive is applied, since its application depends heavily on the institutional environment in which the companies operate (Hamann et al., 2009).

The coercive power of the CSDDD lies not only in its direct legal requirements but also in the broader system of sanctions, liabilities, and market restrictions that could result from non-compliance. The compliance mechanism explains how legal obligations and the threat of sanctions force companies to integrate HRDD into their governance structures to avoid regulatory penalties and market exclusion.

Companies face tangible financial costs, including potential fines, civil liability, and business restrictions, as well as intangible costs, such as reputational damage, loss of legitimacy, and exclusion from socially sensitive markets (Leite et al., 2024; Litwin & Savourey, 2025). A breach of the CSDDD can, therefore, not only result in regulatory sanctions, but also undermine stakeholder confidence, jeopardise access to resources, and undermine long-term competitiveness. Furthermore, the introduction of the CSDDD is likely to have spillover effects beyond the borders of the EU. Companies headquartered in regions where HRDD obligations are required by law are likely to strengthen and formalise their due diligence systems to demonstrate compliance (Lafarre & Rombouts, 2022). At the same time, global companies may adopt similar standards to avoid legal fragmentation and maintain access to EU markets (Neri-Castracane et al., 2024). This leads to an institutional diffusion effect, where coercive pressures in one jurisdiction can indirectly influence practices across borders through supply chain dynamics and competitive benchmarking (Lopatta et al., 2023). In line with institutional theory, it can therefore be expected that companies located in jurisdictions with stronger pressures, such as those headquartered in the EU or in countries where HRDD obligations are already mandatory, show a higher propensity to adopt and improve HRDD practices compared to companies operating in less regulated institutional environments (Christ et al., 2019). Consequently, the present hypothesis is shown:

H1: *Firms headquartered in the EU or in countries with mandatory HRDD regulations will improve their HRDD performance more significantly after 2024, compared to firms in jurisdictions without such rules.*

Based on institutional theory, companies characterised by a higher degree of internationalisation are exposed to heterogeneous pressures from different actors, including consumers, media, governments, and regulatory institutions operating in different national and geographical contexts (Hamann et al., 2009). This multiple exposure makes such companies particularly vulnerable: a bad opinion or scandal in a single country can quickly spread globally through the media, affecting their reputation and, consequently, their economic performance in multiple markets simultaneously (Colovic et al., 2019). Multinational companies, in particular, have always been under public scrutiny, as they are often considered to be the main perpetrators of human rights violations related to environmental abuses, precarious labour conditions or grievances in global supply chains (Wang et al., 2024). For this reason, they find themselves in a position where social legitimacy needs to be constantly renewed and strengthened by applying HRDD practices as a tool to reduce reputational risks and ensure compliance with legal and social expectations. Kostova and Zaheer (1999) and Kostova et al. (2008) emphasise that multinational companies can be defined as genuine institutional carriers, as they operate under the dual influence of the institutions of their country of origin and the institutions of their host countries (Giuliani et al., 2023). This exposes them to a complex system of pressures that force them to adopt common standards and practices, not only to meet local requirements, but also to harmonise their activities globally and maintain internal coherence. Through an imitative channel, companies exposed to multiple institutional contexts adopt HRDD practices by replicating standards of leading peers to reduce uncertainty and maintain coherence across jurisdictions. In the specific context of HRDD, the main binding and non-binding standards have been developed with a particular focus on multinational enterprises and those with the highest degree of internationalisation. This is because these companies face the most complex challenges in managing supply chains that span multiple legal, institutional, and cultural contexts, often characterised by very heterogeneous standards in terms of human rights and sustainability (Ciravegna & Nieri, 2022). In line with the regulatory and mimetic pressures described by institutional theory, the following hypothesis can be presented:

H2a: *Firms' internationalisation is positively related to HRDD practices.*

Companies often tend to adopt certain behaviours or increase the quantity and quality of sustainability information disclosed to align their performance with the best in class in the industry or to protect their reputation from potential reputational and legitimacy risks. In this sense, the introduction of coercive regulations can act as a catalyst, pushing even companies that are less exposed to direct risks or stakeholder pressure to adopt compliant behaviour and resort to forms of mimetic isomorphism to preserve the legitimacy of the organisation (Nicolò et al., 2025). Such a dynamic can set in motion a virtuous cycle of dissemination of HRDD practices and contribute to a convergence towards common standards, even in the absence of formal legal obligations (Romito et al., 2025). The professionalisation mechanism plays a part in this case because HRDD is integrated into sector-wide norms and benchmarks and professional guidelines, and companies incorporate it into their responsible activities.

However, the literature also points to a significant risk: that of purely symbolic or formal compliance, where practices are only superficially implemented and not integrated into corporate culture and values (Buhmann, 2018; Oliver, 1991; Hess, 2021). This raises questions about the actual effectiveness of HRDD practices introduced in response to imitation pressures, which may be limited to fulfilling external expectations without bringing about significant changes in business processes (Ciravegna & Nieri, 2022). In light of the considerations of institutional theory, in particular the concept of mimetic isomorphism, the following research hypothesis is formulated:

H2b: *A higher average industry human rights performance is positively related to HRDD practices.*

The second theoretical framework is the theory of legitimacy, which goes back to the concept of organisational legitimacy. This theory is based on the epistemological assumption that organisations do not operate in a vacuum, but are social entities deeply rooted in a broader context composed of shared norms, values, beliefs, and expectations (Chen & Roberts, 2010; Nicolò et al., 2025). From this perspective, organisational structures are continuously shaped, changed, and redefined through the interaction between companies and society.

According to Suchman's (1995) classic definition, legitimacy can be understood as the "generalised perception or presumption that an entity's actions are desirable, appropriate or congruent with the system of socially constructed norms, values, beliefs and definitions". It, therefore, represents a fundamental intangible resource for companies: The more a company is seen as legitimate, the greater its ability to obtain resources from the external environment, attract investors, maintain stable relationships with stakeholders, and ensure its survival (Deegan & Rankin, 1996). Conversely, non-compliance with the so-called social contract, understood as the set of implicit (norms, customs) and explicit (laws, regulations) expectations that bind the company to society, can undermine the very existence of the company (Dowling & Pfeffer, 1975; Deegan, 2002).

Maintaining legitimacy, therefore, requires companies to respond proactively or reactively to pressure from interest groups, the media, institutions, and public opinion. According to Savage et al. (2001), the higher the likelihood of negative evaluation by society, the greater the propensity of companies to change their behaviour or adopt strategic communication practices to restore a positive image (Oliver, 1991; O'Donovan, 2002). In this sense, legitimacy theory and institutional theory are closely related in that both explain how companies adapt to external pressures to gain social acceptance. However, while institutional theory focuses on isomorphism, legitimacy theory emphasises the link between social perception and organisational survival (DiMaggio & Powell, 1983).

In line with this theory, legitimacy forces drive enhanced HRDD practices through reputation management mechanism: companies facing stakeholder scrutiny, media pressure, or reputational damage from past violations adopt HRDD to restore trust and maintain social license to operate (McPhail & Ferguson, 2025; Wang et al., 2024). A high level of stakeholder engagement increases the visibility and intensity of the societal expectations to which the company is exposed and makes it more difficult to ignore demands related to social responsibility and respect for human rights (Elbel et al., 2023; Avant et al., 2023; Olsen et al., 2025). In this context, the adoption of HRDD practices represents a strategic response to the need to maintain legitimacy, reduce the risk of negative perceptions, and strengthen the relationship of trust with stakeholders (Giuliani et al., 2023). Indeed, direct engagement facilitates a process of mutual accountability: on the one hand, stakeholders exert pressure on the company to act in a socially responsible manner; on the other hand, the company uses tools such as HRDD to demonstrate its commitment, transparency, and compliance with the social contract (Cosa, 2025). In addition, as required by UNGPs and CSDDD, dialogue and consultation with stakeholders is a fundamental pillar of HRDD (Litwin & Savourey, 2025; Wilhelm, 2024). Therefore, in line with previous research findings, a higher level of stakeholder interaction is expected to be positively correlated with the implementation of HRDD practices, as shown by the following hypothesis:

H3a: *Firms' stakeholder engagement is positively related to HRDD practices.*

According to Oliver (1991), the theory of legitimacy is inseparable from the theory of institutions. In fact, it holds that the more a company is exposed to public opinion, the more it is in favour of maintaining its legitimacy (O'Donovan, 2002). Several studies in the broad field of sustainability have shown that companies exposed to greater scrutiny by social and political actors, such as NGOs or other stakeholders, or operating in sectors considered sensitive, can increase their sustainable practices, due diligence and disclosure to improve stakeholder perceptions and maintain their legitimacy (Cho & Patten, 2007; Flynn, 2020; Nicolò et al., 2025). For example, Preuss and Brown (2012) and Lopatta et al. (2023) have observed that companies operating in sectors that are considered sinful are more proactive in communicating their commitment to human rights to avoid stakeholder mobilisation. In addition, Patten (2002) has shown that companies respond to negative performance with increased disclosure to offset the risk of negative external perception. According to Savage et al. (2001), media news is also an indicator of social norms and values and, therefore, poses a potential threat to the legitimacy of the organisation if it is negative. In line with these contributions, the following hypothesis is presented.

H3b: *Firms' media exposure is positively related to HRDD practices.*

According to legitimacy theory, a company that suffers a loss of legitimacy due to negative events tends to use corrective strategies to restore its social acceptance. In the case of human rights violations, such events create significant reputational risk, undermine stakeholder trust, and can jeopardise access to key resources (Romito et al., 2025). In this context, the introduction of HRDD practices can serve as a strategy to restore legitimacy: by introducing systematic prevention, monitoring, and remediation measures, the company signals its commitment not to repeat misconduct and to realign itself with societal expectations. This behaviour is consistent with studies showing that companies respond to negative performance with increased disclosure or stricter sustainability practices to compensate for the loss of legitimacy (Patten, 2002; Cho & Patten, 2007). Therefore, companies that have committed human rights violations in the past have a greater incentive to adopt HRDD as a tool to restore their credibility and re-establish the social contract with their stakeholders. Thus, the following hypothesis is presented:

H3c: *Firms with a history of human rights violations are more likely to adopt HRDD.*

The conceptual model is represented in Fig. 4.1. The upper part represents the institutional pressures, coercive, mimetic, and normative, that drive HRDD adoption, while the lower part captures the legitimacy mechanism, represented by

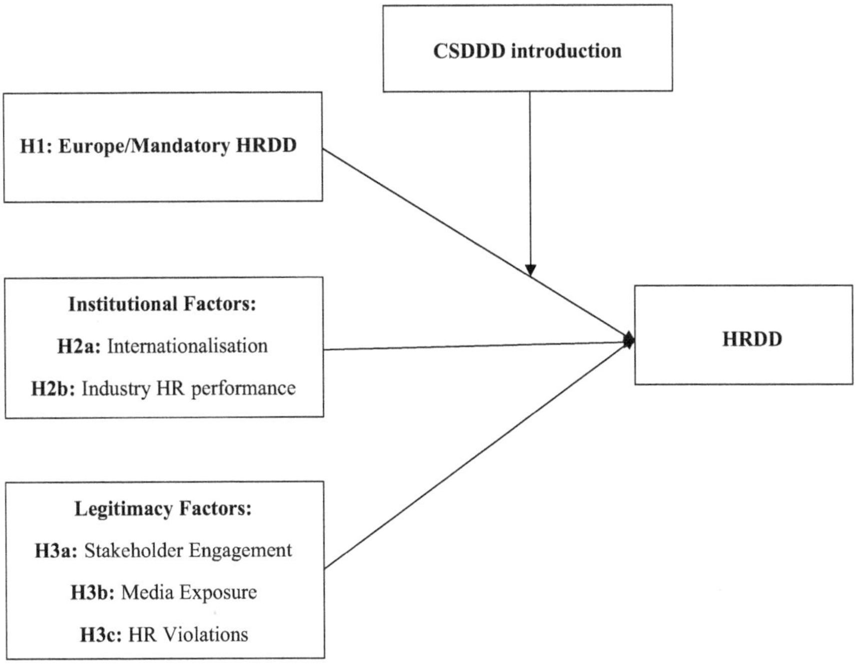

Fig. 4.1 Conceptual model. *Source*: Author's own elaboration

stakeholder engagement, media exposure, and past human rights violations. The CSDDD is positioned as an element that amplifies these pressures, especially for European companies and those operating in countries with pre-existing HRDD regulations.

4.4 Methodology

4.4.1 Sample and Data

To test the research hypotheses, I focused on global companies that are part of the S&P 1200 from 2016 to 2024. The selection of companies belonging to this stock index is done for the following reasons. First, the index includes companies from around the world, which permits the comparison of companies from different regulatory and geographic contexts to determine the potential impact of CSDDD implementation. Secondly, the companies included in this index are large companies, and most of them are also multinational companies operating in different countries. This characteristic helps to evaluate companies that fall within the scope of the directive or are interested in it due to the size of their activities. Thirdly, the index is based on a mix of industries so that a comparison can be made between more sensitive industries and

Table 4.1 Sample selection procedure

Step	Companies	Observations
Initial sample	1220	8943
Observation with missing values	–	(3918)
Final sample	868	5025

Source: Author's own elaboration

those that are less exposed to human rights risk. The original sample comprised 1220 companies and 8943 observations. Missing values were addressed by applying list-wise deletion, whereby all observations with at least one missing value across the variables included in the analysis were removed. This procedure resulted in the exclusion of 3918 observations, yielding a final sample of 5025 company-year observations across 868 companies. All data used in the study are from the LSEG Refinitiv database. The sample construction process is shown in Table 4.1.

4.4.2 *Variables Measurement*

4.4.2.1 Dependent variable

The dependent variable of this study is the Human Rights Due Diligence Score (HRDD Perc), which is a composite measure of a company's implementation of HRDD practices derived from previous literature. The HRDD Perc is determined by adapting the percentile rank methodology used by Palea et al. (2023) to the specific indicators selected to best represent HRDD. The selection of indicators is inspired by literature, more specifically, the use of binary indicators, which treat disclosure as a proxy of policy adoption, follows Principale (2023), while the operationalisation of HRDD as a multidimensional composite score is taken by Torelli et al. (2024) and by García-Sánchez et al. (2025). It consists of ten binary indicators, each coded 1 if the company fulfils a certain criterion or discloses a certain practice, and 0 otherwise. These indicators capture several dimensions of the HRDD process, in accordance with the UNGPs and leading international standards. For each observation of a company year, the sum of the ten binary indicators (from 0 to 10) is converted into a percentile rank relative to all companies in the sample for that year. The resulting HRDD percentile score, therefore, ranges from 0 to 1, with higher values indicating better HRDD performance compared to industry peers over the same period. The components of the HRDD percentile score are presented in Table 4.2.

Table 4.2 Components of HRDD percentile score

Components of HRDD percentile score	
Commitment on Human Rights	The company's explicit commitment to international instruments protecting human rights.
Embedding Human Rights	The company's human rights commitments are made clear to all stakeholders, and whether staff are made aware of their roles and responsibilities in ensuring the company's activities do not result in any violation of human rights.
Grievance Mechanisms Human Rights	It represents a formal system put in place to address and handle complaints or violations related to human rights.
Human Rights Identification	Salient, industry, or business-specific human rights refer to the fundamental rights that are particularly relevant and impactful within a specific industry or business context.
Human Rights Responsibility	A clear process of assigning daily tasks and necessary resources to relevant departments for the supervision and protection of human rights, as an indication of the level of importance the company places on the implementation of its human rights commitments.
Human Rights Stakeholder Engagement	It represents the ongoing engagement with affected stakeholders to address and uphold human rights concerns and interests.
Impact Assessment Human Rights	Given that human rights impacts may change over time, ongoing risk assessment is required to enable a company to keep up to date with changes in the risk environment and incorporate them into its assessments of its salient human rights issues over time.
Internal Human Rights Training	Training on human rights policy represents the process of educating the employees on their roles and responsibilities in ensuring the company's activities do not result in any violation of human rights.
Mitigation of Human Rights Issues	It represents the action taken in response to the ongoing human rights risk assessment carried out by the company.
Human Rights Policy	Does the company have a policy for the exclusion of child, forced or compulsory labour, or to guarantee the freedom of association universally applied, independent of local laws?

Source: Author's own elaboration

4.4.2.2 Dif-in-dif Variables

To test the first hypothesis (H1), two main variables are employed. The first "Europe" is a dummy variable equal to 1 if the company belongs to a European country and 0 otherwise. This variable represents the treatment group, so firms coded as EUROPE = 1 are considered to be within the treatment group for the difference in difference (DiD) model, as they are directly addressed or operating under legal frameworks equivalent to the CSDDD. The second variable is "Post 2024", which is a dummy variable equal to 1 when the year of analysis is 2024 and 0 otherwise. This year represents the cut-off point because it marks the introduction of the CSDDD directive in the European context. The product of the EUROPE and Post 2024 dummies represents the treatment effect of interest in the DiD, event study, and panel regression models.

4.4.2.3 Independent Variables

The independent variables used in the panel regression models were divided into two groups according to the theoretical framework. The first group includes three variables that explain the potential role of institutional theory. These are "Mandatory human rights due diligence laws" (mHRDD), "International sales" (INT SALES%) and "Mean human rights rating" (Mean HR)". The first variable is a dummy variable that takes the value 1 if the company operates in a country where there is a human rights due diligence regulation, that is, "France", "Germany", "Norway", "Netherlands", "Switzerland", "United Kingdom", and 0 otherwise. This variable explains the coercive pressure (Nampoothiri et al., 2024). The second variable is a continuous variable that expresses the percentage of international sales in total sales, explaining both mimetic and normative pressure (Ciravegna & Nieri, 2022; Giuliani et al., 2023). The third variable is the average human rights value per sector and year. It expresses the normative pressure (García-Sánchez et al., 2025).

The second group of control variables belongs to legitimacy theory. The variables are "Stakeholder Engagement Score" (STAK ENG SCORE), "Sector Media Exposure" (MEDIA EXP.), and "Violations of Human Rights" (HR VIOL.). The first variable measures the extent of knowledge about the involvement of interest groups in decision-making processes on a scale of 0–100 (Cosa, 2025). The second variable has a value of 1 for high-risk sectors ("energy", "materials", "Consumer Discretionary"), 2 for medium-risk sectors ("industry", "consumer staples", "healthcare", "utilities"), and 3 for low-risk sectors ("information technology", "communication services", "finance", "real estate"). It indicates the potential risk posed by the media (especially NGOs) due to the specific characteristics of the sectors (Ciravegna & Nieri, 2022; Giuliani et al., 2023). Finally, the third variable is a dummy variable that has a value of 1 if the company discloses incidents of human rights violations and a value of 0 otherwise (García-Sánchez et al., 2025).

4.4.2.4 Control Variables

To improve the explanatory power of the model, the following control variables are included: ESG score, which measures a company's environmental, social and governance performance on a scale between 0 and 100 (Lopatta et al., 2023; Principale, 2023), return on assets (ROA), which is a common measure of a company's profitability (Ciravegna & Nieri, 2022; Giuliani et al., 2023; Cosa, 2025; Principale, 2023; Torelli et al., 2024) and Firm Size (FIRM SIZE), measured as the natural logarithm of the total assets of the companies (Giuliani et al., 2023; Cosa, 2025; Principale, 2023; Torelli et al., 2024; Moussa et al., 2023). The explanation of the variables used in the study is shown in Table 4.3.

Table 4.3 Description of variables

Name	Code	Description	Source	Author(s)
Human Rights Due Diligence Score	HRDD PERC.	Percentile ranking methodology applied to the following variables related to HRDD: "Commitment on Human Rights", "Embedding Human Rights", "Grievance Mechanisms Human Rights", "Human Rights Identification", "Human Rights Responsibility", "Human Rights Stakeholder Engagement", "Impact Assessment Human Rights", "Internal Human Rights Training", "Mitigation Human Rights Issues", "Human Rights Policy".	Author's own elaboration starting from LSEG data	García-Sánchez et al. (2025), Palea et al. (2023), Principale (2023), Torelli et al. (2024)
Mean Human Rights Score	Mean HR	Sectoral mean of the measure of the effectiveness of a company in respecting fundamental human rights conventions.	LSEG	García-Sánchez et al. (2025).
Violations of Human Rights	HR. VIOL.	Dummy variable equal to 1 if the company disclose incidents of human rights violations and 0 otherwise.	LSEG	Romito et al. (2025), Giuliani et al. (2023), Ciravegna and Nieri (2022)
Europe	EUROPE	Dummy variable equal to 1 if the firm belongs to European countries and 0 otherwise.	Author's own elaboration	García-Sánchez et al. (2025)
Post-2024	Post-2024	Dummy variable equal to 1 if the year of analysis is 2024 and 0 otherwise	Author's own elaboration	Lafarre and Rombouts (2022)
Mandatory laws about Human Rights Due Diligence	mHRDD	Dummy variable equal to 1 if the firm belongs to a country in which mandatory rules about HRDD are present and 0 otherwise ("France", "Germany", "Norway", "Netherlands", "Switzerland", "United Kingdom").	Author's own elaboration	Nampoothiri et al. (2024)

(continued)

Table 4.3 (continued)

Name	Code	Description	Source	Author(s)
Sector Media Exposure	MEDIA EXP.	Value equal to 1 for high exposure sectors ("Energy", Materials", "Consumer Discretionary), 2 for media exposure sectors ("Industrials", "Consumer Staples", "Health Care", "Utilities") and 3 for low exposure sectors (Information Technology", "Communication Services", "Financials", "Real Estate).	Author's own elaboration	Ciravegna and Nieri (2022), Giuliani et al. (2023)
ESG Score	ESG SCORE	Measures on a scale of 0–100 that assesses the overall performance of a company in relation to the environmental, social and governance dimensions.	LSEG	Lopatta et al. (2023), Principale (2023)
Stakeholder Engagement Score	STAK ENG. SCORE	Measure on a scale of 0–100 that assesses the extent of knowledge about stakeholders' inclusion in decision-making processes.	LSEG	Cosa (2025)
Return on Assets	ROA	Ratio of net income to total assets.	LSEG	Ciravegna and Nieri (2022), Giuliani et al. (2023), Cosa (2025), Principale (2023), Torelli et al. (2024), Moussa et al. (2023)
Internationals sales	INT SALES%	International sales percentage of total sales.	LSEG	Ciravegna and Nieri (2022) Giuliani et al. (2023)
Firm size	FIRM SIZE	Natural logarithm of total assets.	LSEG	Giuliani et al. (2023), Cosa (2025), Principale (2023), Torelli et al. (2024), Moussa et al. (2023)

Source: Author's own elaboration

4.4.3 Models' Specification

The study follows a multilevel approach, combining a DiD estimation, an event study, and a series of panel regressions to test the research hypotheses. To test the first hypothesis (H1), a standard DiD model was first estimated, where the dependent variable is HRDD_PERC. The DiD model was chosen because it is a non-experimental method that allows the estimation of the average treatment effect on the treated (ATT) by comparing the difference over time between the control and treatment groups (Romito et al., 2025). The treatment variable is the Europe dummy, while the time variable is the post-2024 dummy. The baseline specification is:

$$HRDD\_PERC_{it} = \beta_0 + \beta_1 EUROPE_i + \beta_2 Post\,2024_t + \beta_3 \left(EUROPE_i * Post\,2024_t\right) + \mu_i + \lambda_t + \varepsilon_{it}$$

where μ_i are firm fixed effects, and λ_t are year fixed effects. The coefficient β_3 captures the (ATT), that is, the change in HRDD performance in the treatment group relative to the control group, post-2024.

The second step is an event study to analyse the dynamic effects of CSDDD over time. In this analysis, the dummy for the period after the entry into force of the Directive is replaced by various year-related dummies that capture the temporal effect around the introduction of the Directive. Both the DiD model and the event study are repeated by replacing the dummy EUROPE with the dummy mHRDD.

The third step is a series of panel regression analyses that include the interaction term (EU-ROPE* Post 2024 and mHRDD*Post 2024) as moderators, first without control variables and then by adding them. This analysis provides a robustness test of the previous models. Finally, additional panel regression models were implemented to test the role of institutional and legitimacy factors on the dependent variable (HRDD PERC) and to test the remaining hypotheses.

$$HRDD\ PERC_{it} = \alpha + \delta_1 Institutional_{it} + \delta_2 Legitimacy_{it} + \gamma X_{it} + \mu_{it} + \lambda_{it} + \varepsilon_{it}$$

where:

- $Institutional_{it}$ includes the variables for H2a and H2b (e.g. International Sales, meanHR).
- $Legitimacy_{it}$ includes the variables for H3a–H3c (e.g. stakeholder engagement, media exposure, HR violations).
- X_{it} is the vector of control variables (ESG Score, ROA and firm size).

Robust standard errors are employed to control heteroskedasticity. The results obtained from these models are presented in the following section.

4.5 Results

4.5.1 Descriptive Statistics

Table 4.4 shows the descriptive statistics of the selected variables. The mean HRDD score (percentile) is 0.34, with values ranging from 0 to 1, indicating significant differences in the companies' due diligence practices (standard deviation = 0.33). The mean HR score is 66.49, indicating a good performance of the selected companies, with a standard deviation of 28.22. However, the proportion of companies that disclose information on human rights violations (HR VIOL.) is very low (mean of 0.09 and standard deviation of 0.27). Nearly 38% of the companies are based in Europe, 17% of them in countries where laws on human rights violations already exist. The average score for the sector's media presence (MEDIA EXP) is close to 2, indicating that most companies have a medium level of exposure to media. The average stakeholder engagement score (STAK ENG SCORE) is quite high (58.15), as is the percentage of international sales (56.06). Finally, regarding the control variables, the selected sample shows a good, sustainable performance, as evidenced by an average ESG score of 68.42, a mean profitability (ROA) of 6.59, and a company size (FIRM SIZE) of 24.73. The third column shows the variance inflation factors (VIF), which are all below the threshold of ten, demonstrating the absence of multicollinearity issues.

Table 4.5 shows the correlation coefficients between the key variables. The dependent variable (HRDD PERC) shows a positive relationship with all variables except media presence, which shows that companies in the sector with low media presence (value equal to 3) have lower values in relation to HRDD. The highest correlation value in relation to the dependent variable is between HRDD PERC and ESG Score, but it is quite low (0.376). In general, the highest correlation value is 0.584 between EUROPE and mHRDD. The correlation matrix shows that there are no multicollinearity problems, as previously demonstrated by the VIF score.

Table 4.4 Descriptive statistics

Variable	Count	VIF	Mean	std	Min	25%	50%	75%	Max
HRDD PERC	5025		0.34	0.33	0.00	0.07	0.16	0.69	1.00
HR SCORE	5025	1.278	66.49	28.22	0.00	51.79	74.40	90.69	99.32
HR VIOL.	5025	1.116	0.09	0.28	0.00	0.00	0.00	0.00	1.00
EUROPE	5025	1.747	0.38	0.49	0.00	0.00	0.00	1.00	1.00
mHRDD	5025	1.531	0.17	0.38	0.00	0.00	0.00	0.00	1.00
MEDIA EXP.	5025	1.152	2.10	0.76	1.00	2.00	2.00	3.00	3.00
ESG SCORE	5025	1.599	68.42	15.13	7.51	60.03	71.02	79.56	95.59
STAK ENG SCORE	5025	1.346	58.15	32.61	0.00	55.56	68.75	82.23	94.34
ROA	5025	1.083	6.59	10.04	−55.24	2.07	5.28	9.43	236.78
INT SALES%	5025	1.139	56.06	37.45	0.00	30.96	55.86	82.53	1581.31
FIRM SIZE	5025	1.273	24.73	2.37	17.93	23.11	24.24	25.86	34.17

Source: Author's own elaboration

Table 4.5 Correlation matrix

	(1)	(2)	(3)	(4)	(5)	(6)	(7)	(8)	(9)	(10)	(11)	(12)
(1) HRDD PERC	1											
(2) EUROPE	0.126***	1										
(3) Post_2024	0.0982***	0.0912***	1									
(4) mHRDD	0.133***	0.584***	0.0619***	1								
(5) INT. SALES	0.129***	0.325***	0.0340*	0.210***	1							
(6) MEAN HR	0.218***	0.100***	0.265***	0.0822***	0.113***	1						
(7) STAK. ENG.	0.203***	0.0363*	0.0237	0.0455**	0.0200	0.157***	1					
(8) MEDIA EXP.	−0.0953***	−0.0713***	−0.0262	−0.0719***	−0.123***	−0.322***	−0.0965***	1				
(9) HR VIOL	0.368***	0.180***	0.201***	0.142***	0.0967***	0.207***	0.0723***	−0.0698***	1			
(10) ESG Score	0.376***	0.234***	0.0514***	0.172***	0.134***	0.222***	0.493***	−0.0903***	0.183***	1		
(11) ROA	0.00692	−0.0155	0.00823	−0.0551***	0.00686	−0.00316	−0.0607***	0.0184	0.0179	−0.0844***	1	
(12) FIRM SIZE	0.182***	−0.169***	−0.0239	−0.0982***	−0.0516***	−0.0128	0.193***	0.107***	0.0144	0.289***	−0.257***	1
N. Obs.	5025											

Source: Author's own elaboration. Note: *p<0.1, **p<0.05, ***p<0.01

Table 4.6 shows the distribution of the number of companies and the mean HRDD percentile value per year, country, and sector. Looking at the first panel

Table 4.6 Distribution of HRDD percentile score

	Abs frequency	Rel. frequency (%)	Mean HRDD perc.
Year			
2016			0.25
2017			0.20
2018			0.28
2019			0.33
2020			0.31
2021			0.30
2022			0.46
2023			0.46
2024			0.48
Country			
Australia	28	3.23	0.35
Austria	3	0.35	0.15
Belgium	4	0.46	0.48
Brazil	10	1.15	0.45
Canada	43	4.95	0.22
Chile	7	0.81	0.20
China	9	1.04	0.24
Colombia	2	0.23	0.32
Denmark	11	1.27	0.33
Finland	11	1.27	0.35
France	38	4.38	0.55
Germany	38	4.38	0.54
Hong Kong	5	0.58	0.28
Ireland	18	2.07	0.17
Italy	11	1.27	0.52
Japan	83	9.56	0.36
Korea	12	1.38	0.36
Luxembourg	2	0.23	0.16
Mexico	8	0.92	0.35
Netherlands	27	3.11	0.29
New Zealand	1	0.12	0.04
Norway	6	0.69	0.30
Peru	1	0.12	0.09
Portugal	3	0.35	0.50
Singapore	5	0.58	0.30
Spain	15	1.73	0.29
Sweden	30	3.46	0.30

(continued)

Table 4.6 (continued)

	Abs frequency	Rel. frequency (%)	Mean HRDD perc.
Switzerland	38	4.38	0.30
Taiwan	9	1.04	0.54
UK	70	8.06	0.41
US	320	36.87	0.29
Sector			
Communication Services	45	5.18	0.31
Consumer Discretionary	100	11.52	0.42
Consumer Staples	74	8.53	0.39
Energy	37	4.26	0.45
Financials	131	15.09	0.27
Health Care	93	10.71	0.33
Industrials	168	19.35	0.29
Information Technology	104	11.98	0.35
Materials	72	8.29	0.31
Real Estate	20	2.30	0.22
Utilities	24	2.76	0.41

Source: Author's own elaboration

(temporal distribution), we can see a development path over time, with an initial HRDD percentile value of 0.25 in 2016, which decreased to 0.20 in 2017. After this year, it began to grow, reaching a peak of 0.48 in 2024. Between 2021 (value of 0.30) and 2022, there was a major development with a value of 0.46, which remained stable until 2023. This development is in line with the legal framework, in particular due to the introduction of the CSDDD proposal in 2022. The second panel (country distribution) shows how the S&P 1200 is geographically composed. The majority of companies (36.87%) are from the US, followed by Japanese (9.56%) and UK (8.06%). Other countries are only represented by a limited number of companies; however, the European Union is well represented with 38% of the sample. In contrast, developing countries are barely present, except China and Brazil (1.04% and 1.15% of the sample, respectively). The least represented countries are New Zealand and Peru, with only one company. The analysis of the mean HRDD percentile value per country shows that the best performance is achieved in France (0.55), followed by Taiwan (0.54), Germany (0.54), and Italy (0.52). In contrast, Austria (0.14), Peru (0.09), and New Zealand (0.04) perform worst in terms of HRDD. Finally, the last panel describes the sector distribution in the sample. Almost 20% of the companies in the sample operate in the industrial sector (19.35%), followed by financials (15.09%) and consumer discretionary (11.52%), while the least represented sectors are energy, utilities, and real estate with shares of 4.26%, 2.76%, and 2.30%, respectively. Companies from the energy sector have the highest HRDD percentile, with a mean value of 0.45, followed by cyclical consumer goods and utilities, with mean values of 0.42 and 0.41. Instead, companies from the industrial sector (0.29), the financial sector (0.27), and the property sector (0.22) perform the worst.

4.5.2 *Dif-in-Dif and Event Study*

In the first step of the empirical analysis to test the research hypotheses, a DiD analysis was carried out. The results are shown in Table 4.7. Two models were performed to test how the introduction of CSDDD affects the HRDD practices of the companies in the sample. Both models include control variables such as ESG score, Firm Size, and ROA. In the first model (1), the dummy variable EUROPE is used as a treatment variable, which takes the value 1 for companies based in Europe and 0 otherwise. This is because, according to the existing literature, these companies are subject to greater institutional pressure as they are the main target groups of the Directive. The dummy variable Post_2024 was chosen as the time variable, which takes the value 1 if the year of analysis is 2024, the year in which the Directive formally entered into force, and 0 otherwise. The coefficient estimated by the DiD model is 0.104 and is statistically significant at 5% ($p = 0.019$), confirming that European companies experienced an average increase in HRDD practices of 10.4% after 2024 compared to non-European companies, all other factors remaining equal. The increase in HRDD percentile variables is greater in the treated group (EUROPE) than in the control group, confirming the positive and significant role of CSDDD on human rights due diligence.

To further check the robustness of the results obtained, a second DiD model (2) was run in which the time variable remains unchanged but the treatment variable is mHRDD, that is, a dummy with a value of 1 if the companies operate in countries that have already adopted mandatory HRDD regulations (including France, Germany, Norway, the Netherlands, Switzerland and United Kingdom). The results show a DiD coefficient of 0.101, significant at 5% ($p = 0.040$). Again, the treated companies show a better performance even before the reform, but a higher increase

Table 4.7 DiD results

	(1)	(2)
Post_2024	0.0769**	0.114***
	(0.0335)	(0.0256)
mHRDD		0.104***
		(0.0125)
EUROPE	0.0753***	
	(0.00974)	
DiD	0.104**	0.101**
	(0.0442)	(0.0489)
Constant	0.300***	0.310***
	(0.00595)	(0.00516)
Observations	5025	5025
Control variables	Yes	Yes
R-squared	0.02	0.06

Source: Author's own elaboration. Standard errors in parentheses
Note: *p<0.1, **p<0.05, ***p<0.01

Table 4.8 Event study results

	HRDD_percentile	
	(1)	(2)
Event-3	−0.0203	
	(0.0219)	
Event-2	−0.0407	
	(0.0222)	
Event-1	0.175***	
	(0.0165)	
Event+1	0.186***	
	(0.0232)	
Hrdd-3		0.0187
		(0.0324)
Hrdd-2		−0.00123
		(0.0327)
Hrdd-1		0.186***
		(0.0232)
Hrdd+1		0.247***
		(0.0320)
Constant	−0.553***	−0.552***
	(0.0457)	(0.0458)
Observations	5025	5025
Control var.	YES	YES
R-squared	0.175	0.166
F	221.9***	201.7***

Note: Standard errors in parentheses. The first model adopts the EUROPE dummy as an interaction element, while mHRDD is used as an interaction in the following model. *Source*: Author's own elaboration. *p<0.05, **p<0.01, ***p<0.001

after the directive came into force. These results show that the country's legal framework is an important factor facilitating the introduction and acceleration of due diligence obligations in response to the Directive. A comparison of the two models shows that both lead to results consistent with hypothesis 1 (H1), but that the second model has a lower coefficient than the first, indicating a less pronounced difference. Nevertheless, this model is more refined as it distinguishes between EU countries and countries that already have HRDD regulations without considering the geographical context.

The second step of the analysis consists of conducting two event studies to complete the DiD models. The results are presented in Table 4.8. These models allow us to analyse the temporal evolution of the HRDD percentile variable before and after the introduction of the Directive, with 2023 as the reference year. Both models use control variables (ESG, Firm Size, and ROA). In the first model, the effect of the interaction between the dichotomous variable EUROPE and the years before the Directive (2020-2021-2022) and the year of its entry into force (2024) is observed, represented, respectively, by the variables Event-3, Event-2, Event-1, Event+1. The results of Model 1 show that the coefficients for the years 2020 and 2021 are not significant, confirming the absence of pre-trends. For the year 2022, there is a significant increase in the HRDD percentile variable, indicating a potential anticipation of change by companies in the European context. In 2024, the year in which the Directive formally entered into force, the impact is more pronounced, which is consistent with hypothesis H1, according to which the introduction of the CSDDD has encouraged the adoption of more robust due diligence obligations. The second model uses the variable mHRDD as the treatment group, so that the independent variables in the model are the result of the interaction between this variable and the years before the directive came into force (Hrddd-3, Hrdd-2, Hrdd-1) and 2024 (Hrdd+1). Also in this second model, the results confirm the absence of significant pre-trends, while a positive effect can already be observed in 2022 and a more significant increase in 2024, suggesting that the existence of national regulations has increased the adoption of the due diligence obligations required by the Directive.

4.5.3 Regression Results

The third step of the analysis consists of a series of fixed-effects panel regressions as a robustness check of the DiD models and event studies, and to test additional research hypotheses regarding the impact of institutional and legitimacy factors on HRDD practices. Table 4.9 presents four panel models with interaction. Models 1 and 3 only present the interactions between the 2024-time dummy and the EUROPE and mHRDD dummies, respectively, while models 2 and 4 also include control variables (ROA, FIRM SIZE, and ESG SCORE). All models show time effects and firm-level effects, and clustered errors are included to account for heteroscedasticity. Models 1 and 2 show a positive and significant impact of the interaction between Post_2024 and EUROPE, both before and after adding the control variables. These models support hypothesis 1, as well as what has already been demonstrated by previous analyses, namely that European companies show a higher level of HRDD adoption after 2024 than their non-European counterparts. This shows that these companies are more likely to react to new regulations due to increased regulatory and institutional pressure. Similarly, Models 3 and 4 confirm the positive and significant effect of the interaction between the Post_2024 variable and mHRDD, which also confirms the first hypothesis and the analyses conducted previously. In this case, it can be said that companies operating in countries where HRDD regulations already exist show a greater increase in HRDD practices than companies operating in countries that are introducing such regulations for the first time. In terms of control variables, a positive and significant impact is observed for ROA, company size (FIRM SIZE), and sustainable performance (ESG SCORE). To summarise, larger, more profitable, and more sustainable companies have greater resources and reputational incentives to introduce due diligence procedures.

The last part of the analysis comprises three regression models, represented in Table 4.10, aimed at estimating the role of institutional factors (H2a-H2b) and

Table 4.9 Regression results

	HRDD_percentile			
	(1)	(2)	(3)	(4)
EUROPE	0.0725***	0.0465***		
	(0.00963)	(0.00962)		
Post_2024	0.153**	0.120*	0.196***	0.142**
	(0.0691)	(0.0645)	(0.0660)	(0.0616)
EUROPE*2024	0.103**	0.0726*		
	(0.0424)	(0.0395)		
mHRDD			0.0949***	0.0691***
			(0.0122)	(0.0117)
mHRDD*2024			0.0972**	0.0797*
			(0.0469)	(0.0437)
ROA		0.00150***		0.00165***
		(0.000431)		(0.000431)
FIRM SIZE		0.0201***		0.0192***
		(0.00206)		(0.00200)
ESG SCORE		0.00646***		0.00657***
		(0.000310)		(0.000301)
Cons	0.227***	−0.674***	0.232***	−0.657***
	(0.0615)	(0.0763)	(0.0615)	(0.0757)
Year fixed eff.	Yes	Yes	Yes	Yes
Firm fixed eff.	Yes	Yes	Yes	Yes
Observations	5025	5025	5025	5025
R^2	0.108	0.227	0.109	0.229
F	44.12***	98.28***	44.59***	99.71***

Note: Standard errors in parentheses. *Source*: Author's own elaboration. *p<0.1, **p<0.05, ***p<0.01

legitimacy (H3a-H3b) on due diligence practices, while the third model is a combination of the previous two models. The models have an R^2 between 0.20 and 0.27, which means that between 20 and 27% of the variation in the dependent variable is explained by the regressors. Model 1 examines the role of institutional factors on HRDD practices. Consistent with Hypothesis 1 and the previous moderation analysis, we find that the variable mHRDD has a positive influence on the dependent variable. In addition, the results in the table show that the coefficient of the variable INT SALES% is positive and significant, indicating that greater international exposure leads companies to orient themselves towards ethical and sustainable practices, in line with H2a. In relation to hypothesis H2b, it can be seen that the Mean HR variable has a positive and significant influence on the dependent variable, suggesting that companies tend to align with the rest of the sector, as identified by institutional theory. The first model suggests that companies that are subject to binding regulations, have a higher degree of internationalisation, and operate in sectors with higher human rights standards are more likely to engage in HRDD practices, due to coercive, regulatory, and mimetic pressures. The second model, on the other hand,

Table 4.10 Institutional and legitimacy factors

	HRDD_percentile		
	(1)	(2)	(3)
mHRDD	0.0609***		0.0391***
	(0.0115)		(0.0111)
INT SALES%	0.000594***		0.000475***
	(0.000115)		(0.000111)
Mean HR	0.00291***		0.00138
	(0.000795)		(0.000867)
STAK ENG SCORE		0.000186	0.000230
		(0.000141)	(0.000141)
MEDIA EXP		−0.0261***	−0.0185***
		(0.00538)	(0.00612)
VIOL HR		0.327***	0.317***
		(0.0150)	(0.0150)
ESG SCORE	0.00636***	0.00576***	0.00532***
	(0.000303)	(0.000320)	(0.000326)
ROA	0.00204***	0.00173***	0.00186***
	(0.000431)	(0.000413)	(0.000413)
FIRM SIZE	0.0171***	0.0161***	0.0178***
	(0.00193)	(0.00184)	(0.00186)
Const	−0.710***	−0.465***	−0.574***
	(0.0807)	(0.0725)	(0.0812)
Year Fixed Eff.	Yes	Yes	Yes
Firm Fixed Eff.	Yes	Yes	Yes
Observations	5025	5025	5025
R^2	0.205	0.267	0.273
F	92.50***	130.27***	110.49***

Source: Author's own elaboration
Note: Standard errors in parentheses. *p<0.1, **p<0.05, ***p<0.01

analyses the role of legitimacy factors. The results show that the variable STAK ENG SCORE is not significant, which refutes hypothesis H3a and thus suggests that formal stakeholder engagement is not a decisive factor for HRDD. In contrast, the variable MEDIA EXP has a negative and significant influence on the dependent variable, which confirms hypothesis H3b. Greater media exposure (lower MEDIA EXP value) corresponds to greater attention to due diligence in response to reputational risk. Finally, hypothesis H3c is confirmed by empirical evidence, as the VIOL HR variable has a positive and significant impact on the HRDD percentile variable, suggesting that companies that have suffered and reported human rights violations strengthen HRDD as a legitimacy strategy. With regard to the legitimacy factors, the results provide evidence in favour of two of the three hypotheses presented. Concerning the control variables, the results support previous empirical evidence showing a positive impact of ESG SCORE, ROA, and company size on due diligence practices. The following section discusses these findings in light of the theoretical framework presented in Sect. 4.3.

4.6 Discussion

This chapter's research aims to determine the impact of the CSDDD on the HRDD practices adopted by companies, and to what extent. To test this, various techniques are employed to observe any behavioural changes in this regard after 2024, when the legislation is adopted. Additionally, various regression models are tested to ascertain the influence of institutional and legitimacy factors on due diligence practices. The results are interpreted in light of the conceptual background presented in Chap. 3 and the research gaps identified in Chap. 2, enabling a comparison between the theoretically described dynamics and the empirical evidence obtained from the analysis. The initial results indicate an improvement in due diligence practices for companies based in Europe and in countries where HRDD-related regulations already existed before the Directive. These results confirm that geographical and regulatory affiliation are key factors in the adoption of HRDD (Giuliani et al., 2023; Lafarre & Rombouts, 2022). Notably, European companies have higher HRDD scores than their non-European counterparts, which highlights the significant influence of the European government's binding regulatory process (Christ et al., 2022; Flynn & Walker, 2021; Nicolo et al., 2025).

Nevertheless, this anticipatory response also carries risks. While the improvement in HRDD scores observed before the Directive came into full force may reflect genuine preparation, it could also reflect strategic impression management, with companies signalling compliance to investors and stakeholders without fundamentally restructuring their operations. Whether this anticipatory behaviour will result in substantive change or merely cosmetic compliance is an open and urgent question that future research should address once the Directive has been fully transposed into national law.

Similar considerations apply to companies based in countries with mandatory HRDD requirements. The results show that these companies are more likely than others in the sample to increase their due diligence obligations after 2024, that is, after the CSDDD is adopted. The same applies to non-European companies in Switzerland and the United Kingdom, which are not directly subject to the Directive, but could be indirectly affected by it due to their turnover or supply chain. Additionally, the results of the event study indicate that developments in the HRDD perspective occurred in 2022, when the directive was first proposed. The greater involvement of these companies confirms the heterogeneity of application explained in the theoretical framework of the third chapter. Indeed, it is feared that considerable differences between countries will persist even if the regulation is applied throughout Europe. This is undoubtedly due to the heterogeneity of legislation, as well as the level of preparation of companies within each country (Roszkowska-Menkes et al., 2024). Consequently, it can be assumed that the application of the

Directive will differ depending on whether companies come from countries that are new to such legislation or from countries with a longer or shorter tradition in this area. Therefore, the results not only support the fundamental role of regulatory pressure but also explain the possible future differences (Hamann et al., 2009).

Subsequently, the results demonstrate that the implementation of HRDD is influenced not only by coercive measures but also by other institutional factors. For instance, internationalisation is associated with a higher level of HRDD. This can be explained by several factors. Companies operating in different markets are forced to implement more robust HRDD systems to ensure compliance with various jurisdictions. Such companies also face greater international visibility and increased scrutiny from stakeholders and the media, which significantly raises their reputational risk. This forces them to confront regulatory and mimetic pressure to adopt practices and standards in this area (Zagelmeyer, 2020). Finally, the dispersion of supply chains leaves them more exposed to risks relating to human rights violations (Wang et al., 2024). Consequently, empirical evidence shows that internationalisation is an important driver of HRDD, strengthening the legitimacy of companies in global contexts. In conclusion, it can be said that, according to institutional theory, companies tend to align with the rest of their sector. This is demonstrated by the positive impact of the average sector score for human rights on HRDD. In other words, companies operating in sectors where human rights are more widely respected are also the most active in terms of due diligence. This supports the role of mimetic and normative pressure, as it demonstrates that companies tend to adhere to industry standards and emulate the "best in class" in order to mitigate uncertainty regarding their legitimacy (Ciravegna & Nieri, 2022). This will likely be even more true when the Directive comes into force, as there will certainly be a degree of uncertainty in the initial phase. Consequently, less prepared companies will opt for a mimetic strategy to avoid mistakes or unintended offences. Further insights emerge from examining the determinants of HRDD from the perspective of legitimacy theory. This section revealed that media exposure and previous human rights violations influence this practice. As the UNGPs and the CSDDD clearly define, stakeholder engagement is a fundamental step in properly implementing HRDD. It is also a fundamentally important tool for ensuring that the Directive has the desired impact and is not merely applied formally (Cosa, 2025).

However, the results reveal a non-significant relationship that warrants critical reflection. If stakeholder engagement remains largely procedural and confined to consultative processes that do not trigger substantive changes in corporate policies, one of the key pillars of the CSDDD risks becoming ineffective in practice. Companies could report high engagement scores without these translating into meaningful improvements in their due diligence practices, thereby reducing a cornerstone of the Directive to a mere reporting exercise rather than a transformative tool. Therefore, policymakers should consider whether current monitoring mechanisms are sufficient to distinguish genuine stakeholder dialogue from ceremonial compliance.

In contrast, the importance of media exposure is recognised. According to legitimacy theory, companies constantly endeavour to strengthen or maintain their reputation; therefore, greater media exposure can be a very important factor in reinforcing societal expectations (Romito et al., 2025). Consequently, companies that are more exposed to media attention, such as NGOs, may suffer greater reputational and economic damage and, therefore, apply stricter due diligence practices to maintain their social legitimacy (Elbel et al., 2023). Finally, the last decisive factor analysed is the role of previously documented human rights violations. In this case too, the results showing a positive effect of this phenomenon on the dependent variable are in line with legitimacy theory. According to this theory, companies that have reported human rights violations and suffered reputational damage as a result have implemented measures, including HRDD practices, to rebuild stakeholder trust and regain their "social legitimacy to operate" (Romito et al., 2025).

However, this reactive approach raises a critical concern. If companies primarily strengthen their HRDD practices after suffering reputational damage rather than as a preventive measure, then even with binding regulations, the current framework may not be sufficient to shift corporate culture from a damage-control logic to a rights-holder-centred approach. Therefore, the effectiveness of the CSDDD may depend not only on the stringency of its enforcement mechanisms, but also on its ability to incentivise proactive behaviour over reactive behaviour.

4.7 Conclusions

This chapter aims to empirically test the theoretical framework presented in Chap. 3 by examining the role of the CSDDD, a recently implemented legislative measure, in relation to corporate behaviour and HRDD practices. Additionally, the study proposes a set of determinants related to institutional and legitimacy factors that may influence these practices. The results show that companies located in European countries, the direct scope of the Directive, or operating in countries that had previously adopted HRDD regulations, increase their HRDD practices more than the rest of the sample. This behaviour was already evident before the adoption of the Directive, indicating that companies must prepare for compliance with the mandatory regulations. Analysis of the determinants also suggests that companies' adoption of HRDD practices largely depends on the external context, particularly regulatory pressure, the degree of internationalisation of activities, industry standards, media exposure, and previous cases of human rights violations. The study's results offer important implications for both the existing literature and the behaviour of various stakeholders.

From a theoretical perspective, this study makes three key contributions to the existing literature. First, it is one of the earliest empirical studies to quantitatively assess the anticipated impact of the CSDDD on corporate HRDD practices. Unlike previous studies, which have predominantly adopted theoretical or qualitative approaches, this study examines the initial response of companies both within and outside the scope of the Directive, using a large-scale, cross-national sample. In doing so, it moves beyond normative prescriptions to provide concrete empirical evidence of how a binding regulatory intervention can shape corporate behaviour even before it is fully transposed into national law. Secondly, the study makes an original theoretical contribution by integrating institutional theory and legitimacy theory within a quantitative analytical framework. While both theories have been used separately in the sustainability and BHR literature, their combined application to HRDD is underdeveloped. This integration enables the study to capture the full range of factors that influence corporate HRDD adoption, providing a more comprehensive explanatory model than either theory could offer independently. Thirdly, the findings demonstrate that firms respond to regulatory signals ex ante, that is, before the Directive formally enters into force. This contributes to the broader debate on regulatory effectiveness by showing that the mere announcement of binding legislation can trigger anticipatory compliance. This has important implications for how policymakers design and communicate regulatory interventions in the field of corporate sustainability.

From a practical perspective, the results provide policymakers with valuable insights. Firstly, the study illustrates the level of preparedness for the introduction of the CSDDD. The findings suggest that companies are reevaluating the way they perceive and approach HRDD even before the implementation of the Directive. Additionally, the results emphasise that the effectiveness of the Directive will be influenced by various factors, which can be understood through theories related to institutions and legitimacy. Secondly, the lack of influence of stakeholder engagement on HRDD practices suggests that relying exclusively or primarily on stakeholder engagement may not be sufficient to enhance accountability or mitigate risks connected to policy implementation. Thirdly, the analysis shows that companies with greater media exposure and a history of human rights abuses are more likely to adopt HRDD. Public authorities can, therefore, use these aspects to their advantage to establish clear and effective monitoring systems and promote the effective adoption of HRDD.

From a corporate perspective, the results are also useful, as they demonstrate that the adoption of HRDD is not only a means of complying with new legal obligations, but also a strategy for legitimising and managing reputational risk. Secondly, companies with greater visibility who have previously reported violations have a strategic incentive to adopt comprehensive HRDD practices in order to maintain stakeholder trust and the legitimacy of their operations. Thirdly, the study shows that media exposure strongly influences HRDD, meaning transparency of such practices is key for consumers and other stakeholders, including investors, to reward or penalise companies. The same applies to NGOs, who can translate transparency into substantive accountability by working with policymakers to ensure monitoring and enforcement mechanisms.

Overall, the findings paint a comprehensive and nuanced picture of the transformative power of the CSDDD. While the directive is encouraging a trend of anticipatory compliance among European companies and those previously regulated, evidence suggests this is largely driven by external pressures. Consequently, there are concerns that companies are adopting such practices merely to avoid the impact of non-compliance on their operations and costs. If the directive leads to an increase in cosmetic compliance, it risks becoming just another layer of regulation that lacks the capacity to reduce human rights violations. Understanding the CSDDD will require observing not how much companies report on HRDD, but the substantive changes in how they identify, prevent, and remedy human rights issues relating to their activities and value chain. These crucial aspects remain unresolved and may be analysed by researchers and policymakers in the coming years.

Despite its contributions, the study has limitations. It is important to note that the Directive has not yet been fully implemented. Therefore, the findings primarily provide insight into companies' current readiness and the anticipated effects before enforcement. Once the Directive has been transposed into binding national regulations, it will be possible to understand the extent to which it has been adopted and how companies have responded, whether symbolically or substantially. Secondly, as HRDD is a complex concept, while the use of a synthetic score permits analysis of large samples, important aspects may be lost. In future, primary data collected through questionnaires or interviews could mitigate this issue. Finally, the analysis is based on S&P 1200 companies, which represent a large, general sample but do not sufficiently reflect the situation in developing countries or their response to institutional interventions. While the analysis focuses on advanced countries, which are more directly or indirectly affected by the Directive in terms of turnover or value chain, it will be possible in future to conduct a comparative analysis to understand how companies in developing countries fare in relation to the HRDD compared to their counterparts in advanced countries.

Chapter 5
Final Considerations

In a context characterised by recurring corporate scandals and unstable political scenarios, there has been growing attention to the responsibility of businesses and states in protecting human rights and implementing HRDD. In light of this scenario, this dissertation aims to offer a comprehensive and structured contribution to the debate, creating a link between legal, organisational, and managerial perspectives, with a particular focus on the managerial and accounting approach. Starting from the fragmentation of the existing literature, the work analyses the evolution of the regulatory framework and how it concretely affects corporate practices.

The first chapter outlined the state of the art of HRDD research through an SLR. The analysis made it possible not only to identify the main characteristics of existing studies, but also to map the main thematic and methodological strands, highlighting significant gaps in the literature. There was a lack of empirical and quantitative studies, especially longitudinal studies based on global samples, which are useful for understanding how the directives actually influence corporate behaviour.

The second chapter, responding to one of the main research questions that emerged from the SLR, shifted the focus from literature review to a theoretical and conceptual reflection on the foundations of HRDD, its integration into corporate practices, and the institutional change introduced by the CSDDD. Through the lens of institutional theory, according to which companies respond to coercive, mimetic, and regulatory pressures, a theoretical framework was developed that integrates three key elements: institutional pressures, regulation, and corporate practices. This model made it possible to identify the advantages, critical issues, and possible ways of implementing the directive, as well as to highlight the risks of symbolic compliance and possible strategies to mitigate them.

The third chapter, also based on the gaps that emerged from the systematic review, aimed to empirically test the proposed theoretical framework, expanding it through the integration of legitimacy theory. The empirical analysis showed that

I. Mastrorocco, *From Voluntary Responsibility to Regulatory Compliance*, SIDREA Series in Accounting and Business Administration,
https://doi.org/10.1007/978-3-032-34492-2_5

companies operating in more stringent institutional contexts, characterised by high internationalisation and better past performance in human rights, have more advanced levels of HRDD.

At the same time, in line with legitimacy theory, companies that are most exposed to media pressure or have a history of human rights violations tend to significantly strengthen their due diligence practices. This empirical contribution stands out for the size of the sample analysed and the longitudinal approach adopted.

The dissertation has achieved its objective of providing a comprehensive and original contribution to the topic of HRDD from a managerial and accounting perspective. Through a process ranging from systematic literature mapping to theoretical reflection and large-scale empirical verification, the work has connected academic debate, regulatory developments, and corporate practices. The value of the contribution lies not only in the description of the state of the art, but above all in the attempt to propose an interpretative model and verify its empirical validity.

However, some limitations remain, opening up interesting prospects for future research. First, the empirical sample focuses on large internationally listed companies; future analyses could extend the investigation to smaller companies or those operating in emerging contexts.

Furthermore, the theoretical framework could be further enriched through qualitative studies, such as in-depth interviews, which would be useful for exploring the decision-making dynamics and organisational processes underlying the implementation of the legislation. Finally, with the entry into force of the CSDDD and its progressive application in the various Member States, it will be essential to develop longitudinal studies capable of assessing the concrete effects of the directive on businesses and global value chains.

In conclusion, the challenge posed by the HRDD is no longer merely theoretical or regulatory, but eminently practical and strategic. Businesses and stakeholders are called upon to transform formal obligations into concrete, effective, and responsible practices. In the hope that this work will contribute to more integrated research and more rigorous and meaningful reporting, this monograph concludes with the conviction that the real effectiveness of HRDD lies in the dialogue between law, management, and accounting.

References

Aizawa, M., Dos Santos, D. C., & Seck, S. L. (2018). Financing human rights due diligence in mining projects. In S. K. Lodhia (Ed.), *Mining and sustainable development* (pp. 99–122). Routledge. www.routledge.com/series/REISD

Al-Shaer, H., Albitar, K., & Hussainey, K. (2024). Corporate accountability for human rights: Evidence from conflict mineral ratings. *Business and Society, 63*(8), 1887–1936. https://doi.org/10.1177/00076503241254829

Amato-Neto, J., & Amato, L. F. (2019). Brazilian companies' presented at 20th International Annual European Operations Management Association (EurOMA) Conference. *International Journal of Innovation and Sustainable Development, 13*(2).

Amengual, M., Mota, R., & Rustler, A. (2023). The 'Court of Public Opinion:' Public perceptions of business involvement in human rights violations. *Journal of Business Ethics, 185*(1), 49–74. https://doi.org/10.1007/s10551-022-05147-5

Areias, S. A. (2024). Striving for a rapid transition: How companies are approaching integrating respect for human rights in their climate action. *Business and Human Rights Journal*, 1–7. https://doi.org/10.1017/bhj.2024.17

Arni, L., Kermode, Y., Leitz, C., & Seidler, A. (2015). UBS and the integration of human rights due diligence under the United Nations (UN) protect, respect and remedy framework for business and human rights. In K. Wendt (Ed.), *Responsible investment banking risk management frameworks, sustainable financial innovation and soft law standards* (pp. 205–216). Springer. https://doi.org/10.1007/978-3-319-10311-2

Arnold, D. G. (2010). Transnational corporations and the duty to respect basic human rights. *Business Ethics Quarterly, 20*(3), 371–399. https://doi.org/10.5840/beq201020327

Arnold, D. G. (2016). Corporations and human rights obligations. *Business and Human Rights Journal, 1*(2), 255–275. https://doi.org/10.1017/bhj.2016.19

Avant, D., Finn, D., & Olsen, T. D. (2023). Can CSR strategy mediate conflict over extraction? Evidence from two mines in Peru. *World Development, 170*, 1–12. https://doi.org/10.1016/j.worlddev.2023.106323

Avery, C. (2021). Business and human rights in a time of change. In *Liability of multinational corporations under international law* (pp. 17–73). Brill | Nijhoff. https://doi.org/10.1163/9789004482678_003

Barrientos, S., Bianchi, L., & Berman, C. (2019). Gender and governance of global value chains: Promoting the rights of women workers. *International Labour Review, 158*(4), 729–752. https://doi.org/10.1111/ilr.12150

I. Mastrorocco, *From Voluntary Responsibility to Regulatory Compliance*, SIDREA Series in Accounting and Business Administration, https://doi.org/10.1007/978-3-032-34492-2

Baydas, L. (2025). Human rights due diligence within the arms industry: Challenges, practices and opportunities. *Business and Human Rights Journal*, 1–7. https://doi.org/10.1017/bhj.2025.1

Bekefi, T., Jenkins, B., Kytle, B., & Mossavar-Rahmani, T. (2006). *Social risk as strategic risk* (30; Corporate Social Responsibility Initiative). http://www.hks.harvard.edu/m-rcbg/CSRI/

Bernaz, N. (2016). *Business and human rights: History, law and policy—Bridging the accountability gap* (1st ed.). Routledge.

Blanco Vizarreta, C., & Betta, W. (2022). Business and human rights in Latin America: A systematic review of scholarship. *Business and Human Rights Journal, 7*(3), 342–374. https://doi.org/10.1017/bhj.2022.4

Blanton, S. L., & Blanton, R. G. (2006). Human rights and foreign direct investment: A two-stage analysis. *Business & Society, 45*(4), 464–485. https://doi.org/10.1177/0007650306293392

Boele, R., & Crispin, C. (2013). What direction for human rights impact assessments? *Impact Assessment and Project Appraisal, 31*(2), 128–134. https://doi.org/10.1080/14615517.2013.771005

Boersma, M. (2018). Between norms and practice: Civil society perspectives on the legitimacy of multistakeholder initiatives to eliminate child labor. *Business Strategy and the Environment, 27*(5), 612–620. https://doi.org/10.1002/bse.2066

Bonnitcha, J., & McCorquodale, R. (2017). The concept of 'due diligence' in the UN guiding principles on business and human rights. *European Journal of International Law, 28*(3), 899–919. https://doi.org/10.1093/ejil/chx042

Bowen, H. R. (1953). *The social responsibilities of the businessman*. Harper & Row.

Brammer, S., Jackson, G., & Matten, D. (2012). Corporate Social Responsibility and institutional theory: New perspectives on private governance. *Socio-Economic Review, 10*, 3–28.

Bueno, N., Bernaz, N., Holly, G., & Martin-Ortega, O. (2024). The EU directive on corporate sustainability due diligence (CSDDD): The final political compromise. *Business and Human Rights Journal*, 1–7. https://doi.org/10.1017/bhj.2024.10

Buhmann, K. (2017). Chinese human rights guidance on minerals sourcing: Building soft power. *Journal of Current Chinese Affairs, 46*(2), 135–154.

Buhmann, K. (2018). Neglecting the proactive aspect of Human Rights Due Diligence? A critical appraisal of the EU's Non-Financial Reporting Directive as a pillar one avenue for promoting pillar two action. *Business and Human Rights Journal, 3*(1), 23–45. https://doi.org/10.1017/bhj.2017.24

Buhmann, K. (2023). Addressing a human rights paradox in the green transition: Guidance for invested mining operations to benefit local communities. *Journal of Cleaner Production, 419*, 1–10. https://doi.org/10.1016/j.jclepro.2023.137903

Buhmann, K. (2024). Non-financial reporting between information and transformation: Taking a corporate sustainability due diligence approach to advancing sustainable and responsible business conduct. In *The Routledge handbook of accounting for the sustainable development goals* (pp. 97–111). Routledge.

Buhmann, K. (2025). Non-financial reporting between information and transformation: Taking a corporate sustainability due diligence approach to advancing sustainable and responsible business conduct. In A. Venturelli & C. Mio (Eds.), *The Routledge handbook of accounting for the sustainable development goals* (pp. 97–111). Routledge. https://doi.org/10.4324/9781003404118

Buhmann, K., & Feld, L. (2024). Shifting boundaries: A transnational legal perspective on the EU Corporate Sustainability Due Diligence Directive. *Transnational Legal Theory, 15*(3), 370–396.

Buhmann, K., Jonsson, J., & Fisker, M. (2019). Do no harm and do more good too: Connecting the SDGs with business and human rights and political CSR theory. *Corporate Governance, 19*(3), 389–403. https://doi.org/10.1108/CG-01-2018-0030

Burritt, R. L., & Christ, K. L. (2023). Modern slavery and the Global Reporting Initiative – A bridge too far? *Business Strategy & Development, 6*(3), 296–309. https://doi.org/10.1002/bsd2.239

Butt, J. S., & Kousar, F. (2024). Driving sustainable growth: The corporate sustainability due diligence directive as a catalyst (CSDDD) for public administration reform and corporate accountability in the European Green Deal. *Journal of Accounting and Management, 14*(3), 7–25. https://dj.univ-danubius.ro/index.php/JAM/article/view/3107

Cahaya, F. R., & Hervina, R. (2019). Do human rights issues matter? An empirical analysis of Indonesian companies' reporting. *Social Responsibility Journal, 15*(2), 226–243. https://doi.org/10.1108/SRJ-10-2016-0171

Carroll, A. B. (1999). Corporate social responsibility: Evolution of a definitional construct. *Business & Society, 38*(3), 268–295. https://doi.org/10.1177/000765039903800303

Carroll, A. B., & Shabana, K. M. (2010). The business case for corporate social responsibility: A review of concepts, research and practice. *International Journal of Management Reviews, 12*(1), 85–105.

Chen, J. C., & Roberts, R. W. (2010). Toward a more coherent understanding of the organization–society relationship: A theoretical consideration for social and environmental accounting research. *Journal of Business Ethics, 97*(4), 651–665. https://doi.org/10.1007/s10551-010-0531-0

Chen, Y., & Sheehy, B. (2025). Does mandatory corporate human rights due diligence offer a path to resolving global food insecurity challenges? *American University International Law Review, 40*(4), 981–1055. https://digitalcommons.wcl.american.edu/auilr/vol40/iss4/2.

Cho, C. H., & Patten, D. M. (2007). The role of environmental disclosures as tools of legitimacy: A research note. *Accounting, Organizations and Society, 32*(7–8), 639–647. https://doi.org/10.1016/j.aos.2006.09.009

Choudhury, B. (2023). Corporate law's threat to human rights: Why human rights due diligence might not be enough. *Business and Human Rights Journal, 8*(2), 180–196. https://doi.org/10.1017/bhj.2023.29

Christ, L. K., Burrit, R. L., & Prider, H. (2022). Modern slavery disclosures in mining: A comparison of large UK and Australian companies. *Journal of Behavioural Economics and Social Systems, 4*(2), 1–19. https://doi.org/10.54337/ojs.bess.v4i2.7747

Christ, K. L., Rao, K. K., & Burritt, R. L. (2019). Accounting for modern slavery: An analysis of Australian listed company disclosures. *Accounting, Auditing & Accountability Journal, 32*(3), 836–865. https://doi.org/10.1108/AAAJ-11-2017-3242

Ciravegna, L., & Nieri, F. (2022). Business and human rights: A configurational view of the antecedents of human rights infringements by emerging market firms. *Journal of Business Ethics, 179*(2), 431–450. https://doi.org/10.1007/s10551-021-04861-w

Cochrane. 2021. *Cochrane handbook for systematic reviews of interventions version 6.2.* https://training.cochrane.org/handbook/current

Colovic, A., Escobar, O. R., Lamotte, O., & Meschi, P. X. (2019). Multinational enterprises, local firms, and employee human rights violation in the workplace: Evidence from Mexico. *Multinational Business Review, 27*(3), 247–265. https://doi.org/10.1108/MBR-06-2017-0037

Cosa, M. (2025). Do corporate human rights commitments drive real impact? Insights from global benchmark data. *Corporate Social Responsibility and Environmental Management, 32*(3), 4235–4253. https://doi.org/10.1002/csr.3180

Cragg, W. (2012). Ethics, enlightened self-interest, and the corporate responsibility to respect human rights: A critical look at the justificatory foundations of the UN framework. *Business Ethics Quarterly, 22*(1), 9–36. https://doi.org/10.5840/beq20122213

Davaanyam, O., & Krajewski, M. (2025). Articulating responsibility for human rights and the environment in the financial sector: Outlook on the concrete cases of the OECD, national contact points. In O. Davaanyam & M. Krajewski (Eds.), *Exploring corporate human rights responsibilities in OECD case law* (pp. 51–82). https://doi.org/10.1007/978-3-031-75717-4

Deegan, C. (2002). The legitimising effect of social and environmental disclosures – a theoretical foundation. *Accounting, Auditing & Accountability Journal, 15*(3), 282–311. https://doi.org/10.1108/09513570210435852

Deegan, C., & Rankin, M. (1996). Do Australian companies report environmental news objectively? *Accounting, Auditing & Accountability Journal, 9*(2), 50–67. https://doi.org/10.1108/09513579610116358

Dehbi, F., & Martin-Ortega, O. (2023). An integrated approach to corporate due diligence from a human rights, environmental, and TWAIL perspective. *Regulation and Governance, 17*(4), 927–943. https://doi.org/10.1111/rego.12538

Dempere, J., Udjo, E., & Mattos, P. (2024). The entrepreneurial impact of the European Directive on corporate sustainability due diligence. *Administrative Sciences, 14*(10), 1–30. https://doi.org/10.3390/admsci14100266

Dempsey, B. W. (1949). The roots of business responsibility. *Harvard Business Review, 27*(4), 393–404.

Deva, S., & Bilchitz, D. (Eds.). (2013). *Human rights obligations of business: Beyond the corporate responsibility to respect?* Cambridge University Press.

Deva, S., Ramasastry, A., & Wettstein, F. (2023). Beyond human rights due diligence: What else do we need? *Business and Human Rights Journal, 8*(2), 133–134. https://doi.org/10.1017/bhj.2023.33

Di Lorenzo, F. (2018). Mineral supply chain transparency: Soft and hard laws on supply chains due diligence and the rise of public-private partnerships. In *CSR, sustainability, ethics and governance* (pp. 135–144). Springer Nature. https://doi.org/10.1007/978-3-319-63561-3_9

DiMaggio, P. J., & Powell, W. W. (1983). The iron cage revisited: Institutional isomorphism and collective rationality in organizational fields. *American Sociological Review, 48*(2), 147–160.

Dowling, J., & Pfeffer, J. (1975). Organizational legitimacy: Social values and organizational behavior. *The Pacific Socio-Logical Review, 18*(1), 122–136.

Dupont, V., Pietrzak, D., & Verbrugge, B. (2024). A step in the right direction, or more of the same? A systematic review of the impact of human rights due diligence legislation. *Human Rights Review, 25*(2), 131–154. https://doi.org/10.1007/s12142-024-00724-9

Ebert, I., Wildhaber, I., & Adams-Prassl, J. (2021). Big data in the workplace: Privacy due diligence as a human rights-based approach to employee privacy protection. *Big Data and Society, 8*(1), 1–14. https://doi.org/10.1177/20539517211013051

Edelman, L. B. (2016). *Working law courts, corporations, and symbolic civil rights*. The University of Chicago Press.

Elbel, J., Bose O'Reilly, S., & Hrzic, R. (2023). A European Union corporate due diligence act for whom? Considerations about the impact of a European Union due diligence act on artisanal and small-scale cobalt miners in the Democratic Republic of Congo. *Resources Policy, 81*, 1–11. https://doi.org/10.1016/j.resourpol.2022.103241

Emanuilov, I., & Yordanova, K. (2022). Business and human rights in Industry 4.0: A blueprint for collaborative human rights due diligence in the factories of the future. *Journal of Responsible Technology, 10*, 1–16. https://doi.org/10.1016/j.jrt.2022.100028

Escrig-Olmedo, E., Fernández-Izquierdo, M. Á., Ferrero-Ferrero, I., Rivera-Lirio, J. M., & Muñoz-Torres, M. J. (2019). Rating the raters: Evaluating how ESG rating agencies integrate sustainability principles. *Sustainability, 11*(3), 1–16. https://doi.org/10.3390/su11030915

Esoimeme, E. E. (2020). Using the risk-based approach to curb modern slavery in the supply chain: The Anglo American and Marks and Spencer example. *Journal of Financial Crime, 27*(2), 313–322. https://doi.org/10.1108/JFC-05-2019-0056

European Commission. (2011). *A renewed EU strategy 2011–14 for corporate social responsibility*. Accessed March 15, 2025, from https://single-market-economy.ec.europa.eu/industry/sustainability/corporate-sustainability-and-responsibility_en.

European Commission. (2024). *Proposal for a directive on corporate sustainability due diligence (COM(2024) XXX final)*. Publications Office of the European Union. Accessed March 15, 2025, from https://eur-lex.europa.eu/

European Commission. (2025). *Proposal for a directive of the European Parliament and of the Council amending Directives (EU) 2022/2464 and (EU) 2024/1760 as regards the dates from which Member States are to apply certain corporate sustainability reporting and due diligence requirements*. Accessed September 28, 2025, from https://eur-lex.europa.eu/

Fasciglione, M. (2020). Implementing responsible business conduct approaches under the UN guiding principles on business and human rights at the time of COVID-19. *European Papers-A Journal on Law and Integration, 5*(3), 1435–1450. https://doi.org/10.15166/2499-8249/404

Fasterling, B. (2017). Human rights due diligence as risk management: Social risk versus human rights risk. *Business and Human Rights Journal, 2*(2), 225–274. https://doi.org/10.1017/bhj.2016.26

Fasterling, B., & Demuijnck, G. (2013). Human rights in the void? Due diligence in the UN guiding principles on business and human rights. *Journal of Business Ethics, 116*(4), 799–814. https://doi.org/10.1007/s10551-013-1822-z

Favotto, A., & Kollman, K. (2022). When rights enter the CSR field: British firms' engagement with human rights and the UN Guiding Principles. *Human Rights Review, 23*(1), 21–40. https://doi.org/10.1007/s12142-020-00614-w

Flynn, A. (2020). Determinants of corporate compliance with modern slavery reporting. *Supply Chain Management, 25*(1), 1–16. https://doi.org/10.1108/SCM-10-2018-0369

Flynn, A., & Walker, H. (2021). Corporate responses to modern slavery risks: An institutional theory perspective. *European Business Review, 33*(2), 295–315. https://doi.org/10.1108/EBR-05-2019-0092

Ford, J., & Nolan, J. (2020). Regulating transparency on human rights and modern slavery in corporate supply chains: the discrepancy between human rights due diligence and the social audit Australian. *Journal of Human Rights, 26*(1) 27–45. https://doi.org/10.1080/1323238X.2020.1761633

Freeman, R. E. (1984). *Strategic management: A stakeholder approach*. Pitman.

García-Sánchez, I. M., Raimo, N., Vitolla, F., & Aibar-Guzmán, B. (2025). Does human-oriented governance foster labor and human rights disclosure? *Review of Managerial Science*, 1–37. https://doi.org/10.1007/s11846-025-00843-8

Gasser, U. (2007). *Responsibility for human rights violations, acts or omissions, within the sphere of influence of companies*. The Berkman Center for Internet and Society at Harvard Law School Research Publication No. 2007-12.

Giuliani, E., Nieri, F., & Vezzulli, A. (2023). Big profits, big harm? Exploring the link between firm financial performance and human rights misbehavior. *Business and Society, 62*(6), 1248–1299. https://doi.org/10.1177/00076503221144994

Götzmann, N. (2017). Human rights impact assessment of business activities: Key criteria for establishing a meaningful practice. *Business and Human Rights Journal, 2*(1), 87–108. https://doi.org/10.1017/bhj.2016.24

Graetz, G., & Franks, D. M. (2013). Incorporating human rights into the corporate domain: Due diligence, impact assessment and integrated risk management. *Impact Assessment and Project Appraisal, 31*(2), 97–106. https://doi.org/10.1080/14615517.2013.771006

Graf, A., & Iff, A. (2017). Respecting human rights in conflict regions: How to avoid the "conflict spiral". *Business and Human Rights Journal, 2*(1), 109–133. https://doi.org/10.1017/bhj.2016.9

Guix, M., & Lotfy, M. (2025). Doing the right thing? The hotel industry's management of, and reporting on, modern slavery. *Tourism Management, 107*, 1–12. https://doi.org/10.1016/j.tourman.2024.105084

Hamann, R., Sinha, P., Kapfudzaruwa, F., & Schild, C. (2009). Business and human rights in South Africa: An analysis of antecedents of human rights due diligence. *Journal of Business Ethics, 87*(2), 453–473. https://doi.org/10.1007/s10551-009-0293-8

Hamm, B. (2022). The struggle for legitimacy in business and human rights regulation—A consideration of the processes leading to the UN guiding principles and an international treaty. *Human Rights Review, 23*(1), 103–125. https://doi.org/10.1007/s12142-020-00612-y

Heald, M. (1988). *The social responsibilities of business: Company and community, 1900–1960*. Routledge.

Hess, D. (2021). The management and oversight of human rights due diligence. *American Business Law Journal, 58*(4), 751–798. https://doi.org/10.1111/ablj.12197

Hofmann, H., Schleper, M. C., & Blome, C. (2018). Conflict minerals and supply chain due diligence: An exploratory study of multi-tier supply chains. *Journal of Business Ethics, 147*(1), 115–141. https://doi.org/10.1007/s10551-015-2963-z

Hogan, B. F., & Reyes, J. (2023). Downstream human rights due diligence: Informing debate through insights from business practice. *Business and Human Rights Journal, 8*(3), 434–440. https://doi.org/10.1017/bhj.2023.27

Hubers, F., & Thijssens, T. (2023). Protect, respect, remedy, and report? Development of human rights reporting in the context of formal institutional settings. *Corporate Social Responsibility and Environmental Management, 30*(6), 2783–2798. https://doi.org/10.1002/csr.2515

International Labour Organization (ILO). (2025). *International labour standards and human rights*. Accessed March 16, 2025, from https://www.ilo.org/resource/international-labour-standards-and-human-rights

Ioannou, I., & Serafeim, G. (2012). What drives corporate social performance the role of nation-level institutions. *Journal of International Business Studies, 43*(9), 834–864. https://doi.org/10.1057/jibs.2012.26

Ishida, H., & Wada, H. (2017). The implementation of the UN guiding principles into daily business operations and the 2020 Tokyo Olympic and Paralympic Games. *Business and Human Rights Journal, 2*(1), 143–148. https://doi.org/10.1017/bhj.2016.27

Islam, M. A., & McPhail, K. (2011). Regulating for corporate human rights abuses: The emergence of corporate reporting on the ILO's human rights standards within the global garment manufacturing and retail industry. *Critical Perspectives on Accounting, 22*(8), 790–810. https://doi.org/10.1016/j.cpa.2011.07.003

Jabotinsky, H., & Sarel, R. (2025). *Attitudes toward the corporate sustainability due diligence directive: Survey evidence*. SSRN, 1–33. https://doi.org/10.2139/ssrn.5312055

Kach, A. P., Bhakoo, V., McGaughey, F., Boersma, M., Nolan, J., & Lichtman, S. M. (2024). Humanizing supply chains: Turning the spotlight towards remediation in modern slavery scholarship. *Journal of Purchasing and Supply Management, 31*(1–7). https://doi.org/10.1016/j.pursup.2024.100991

Kamminga, M. T. (2016). Company responses to human rights reports: An empirical analysis. *Business and Human Rights Journal, 1*(1), 95–110. https://doi.org/10.1017/bhj.2015.2

Karp, D. J. (2023). Business and human rights in a changing world order: Beyond the ethics of disembedded liberalism. *Business and Human Rights Journal, 8*(2), 135–150. https://doi.org/10.1017/bhj.2023.10

Kemp, D., & Vanclay, F. (2013). Human rights and impact assessment: Clarifying the connections in practice. *Impact Assessment and Project Appraisal, 31*(2), 86–96. https://doi.org/10.1080/14615517.2013.782978

Kiewisch, M. (2025). Navigating the EU corporate sustainability due diligence directive: How multinational enterprises approach regulatory familiarization in the chocolate sector. *Regulation and Governance*. https://doi.org/10.1111/rego.70042

Kostova, T., Roth, K., & Dacin, M. T. (2008). Institutional theory in the study of multinational corporations: A critique and new directions. *Academy of Management Review, 33*(4), 994–1006. https://doi.org/10.2307/20159458

Kostova, T., & Zaheer, S. (1999). Organizational legitimacy under conditions of complexity: The case of the multinational enterprise. *The Academy of Management Review, 24*(1), 64–81. https://doi.org/10.2307/259037

Krajewski, M., Tonstad, K., & Wohltmann, F. (2021). Mandatory human rights due diligence in Germany and Norway: Stepping, or striding, in the same direction? *Business and Human Rights Journal, 6*(3), 550–558. https://doi.org/10.1017/bhj.2021.43

Kraus, S., Breier, M., & Dasí-Rodríguez, S. (2020). The art of crafting a systematic literature review in entrepreneurship research. *International Entrepreneurship and Management Journal, 16*(3), 1023–1042. https://doi.org/10.1007/s11365-020-00635-4

Kriebitz, A., & Lütge, C. (2020). Artificial intelligence and human rights: A business ethical assessment. *Business and Human Rights Journal, 5*(1), 84–104. https://doi.org/10.1017/bhj.2019.28

Lafarre, A., & Rombouts, B. (2022). Towards mandatory human rights due diligence: Assessing its impact on fundamental labour standardising global value chains. *European Journal of Risk Regulation, 13*, 567–583. https://doi.org/10.1017/err.2022.23

Lambooy, T. (2010). Corporate due diligence as a tool to respect human rights. *Netherlands Quarterly of Human Rights, 28*(3), 404–448. https://doi.org/10.1177/016934411002800304

Leite, E., Koporcic, N., & Markovic, S. (2024). Corporate sustainability reporting: Shifting from optional due diligence to mandatory duty. *Business Ethics, the Environment and Responsibility*, 1–8. https://doi.org/10.1111/beer.12753

Li, Z. (2022). Operationalising the UN guiding principles on business and human rights through human rights due diligence: A critical assessment of current states practices. *Academic Journal of Interdisciplinary Studies, 11*(4), 8–21. https://doi.org/10.36941/ajis-2022-0094

Litwin, D. (2023). Business impacts on economic inequality: An agenda for defining related human rights impacts and economic inequality due diligence. *Business and Human Rights Journal, 8*(1), 90–96. https://doi.org/10.1017/bhj.2022.27

Litwin, D., & Savourey, E. (2025). Human rights in EU sustainable finance. *Journal of Financial Regulation, 11*(1), 41–72. https://doi.org/10.1093/jfr/fjaf001

Lombardi, R., & Secundo, G. (2021). The digital transformation of corporate reporting – a systematic literature review and avenues for future research. *Meditari Accountancy Research, 29*(5), 1179–1208. https://doi.org/10.1108/MEDAR-04-2020-0870

Lopatta, K., Tideman, S. A., Scheil, C., & Makarem, N. (2023). The current state of corporate human rights disclosure of the global top 500 business enterprises: Measurement and determinants. *Critical Perspectives on Accounting, 96*, 1–30. https://doi.org/10.1016/j.cpa.2022.102512

Lundan, S. M., & Muchlinski, P. (2012). Human rights due diligence in global value chains. *Progress in International Business Research, 7*, 181–201. https://doi.org/10.1108/S1745-8862(2012)0000007011

Macchi, C. (2021). The climate change dimension of business and human rights: The gradual consolidation of a concept of "Climate Due Diligence". *Business and Human Rights Journal, 6*(1), 93–119. https://doi.org/10.1017/bhj.2020.25

Macchi, C., & Bernaz, N. (2021). Business, human rights and climate due diligence: Understanding the responsibility of banks. *Sustainability, 13*(15), 1–21. https://doi.org/10.3390/su13158391

Maluțan, D., Rusu, T. M., & Eniu, D. (2024). Improving corporate accountability through mandatory human rights and environmental due diligence. *Journal of Research and Innovation for Sustainable Society, 6*(2), 250–262. https://doi.org/10.33727/JRISS.2024.2.28:250-262

Martha, C., & Logahan, J. M. (2016). Human Rights Due Diligence (HRDD) and Human Rights Impact Assessment (HRIA) best practices to Corporate Shared Value (CSV): A case of British Petroleum Tangguh Project in Papua. *Binus Business Review, 7*(3), 221–226. https://doi.org/10.21512/bbr.v7i3.1785

Martin-Ortega, O. (2017). Human rights risks in global supply chains: Applying the UK modern slavery act to the public sector. *Global Policy, 8*(4), 512–521. https://doi.org/10.1111/1758-5899.12501

Martin-Ortega, O. (2018). Public procurement as a tool for the protection and promotion of human rights: A study of collaboration, due diligence and leverage in the electronics industry. *Business and Human Rights Journal, 3*(1), 75–94. https://doi.org/10.1017/bhj.2017.35

Marzi, G., Balzano, M., Caputo, A., & Pellegrini, M. M. (2025). Guidelines for bibliometric-systematic literature reviews: 10 steps to combine analysis, synthesis and theory development. *International Journal of Management Reviews, 27*, 81–103. https://doi.org/10.1111/ijmr.12381

Matthews, L., Silva, M. E., Figueiredo, M. D., & Lai, J. Y. (2025). Towards environmentally just supply chains: From harm reduction to transformative sustainability actions. *International Journal of Operations and Production Management, 45*(3), 733–755. https://doi.org/10.1108/IJOPM-09-2024-0736

McCall-Smith, K., & Rühmkorf, A. (2019). Sustainable global supply chains: From transparency to due diligence. In *Sustainable trade, investment and finance* (pp. 110–128). Edward Elgar. https://doi.org/10.4337/9781788971041.00012

McConnell, L. (2016). Assessing the feasibility of a business and human rights treaty. *International & Comparative Law Quarterly, 66*(1), 143–180.

McCorquodale, R., & Neely, S. (2022). Directors duties and human rights impacts: A comparative approach. *Journal of Corporate Law Studies, 22*(2), 605–639. https://doi.org/10.1080/14735970.2021.2016147

McCorquodale, R., & Nolan, J. (2021). The effectiveness of human rights due diligence for preventing business human rights abuses. *Netherlands International Law Review, 68*(3), 455–478. https://doi.org/10.1007/s40802-021-00201-x

McCorquodale, R., Smit, L., Neely, S., & Brooks, R. (2017). Human rights due diligence in law and practice: Good practices and challenges for business enterprises. *Business and Human Rights Journal, 2*(2), 195–224. https://doi.org/10.1017/bhj.2017.2

McGaughey, F., Voss, H., Cullen, H., & Davis, M. C. (2022). Corporate responses to tackling modern slavery: A comparative analysis of Australia, France and the United Kingdom. *Business and Human Rights Journal, 7*(2), 249–270. https://doi.org/10.1017/bhj.2021.47

McPhail, K., & Ferguson, J. (2016). The past, the present and the future of accounting for human rights. *Accounting, Auditing and Accountability Journal, 29*(4), 526–541. https://doi.org/10.1108/AAAJ-03-2016-2441

McPhail, K., & Ferguson, J. (2025). Ten years of accounting for human rights: A critical review of how practice has evolved and what might come next. In T. Olsen, H. H. Humphrey, J. Schrempf-Stirling, & H. Van Buren III (Eds.), *A research agenda for business and human rights* (pp. 169–186). Elgaronline. https://doi.org/10.4337/9781802208979

Methven O'Brien, C., & Dhanarajan, S. (2016). The corporate responsibility to respect human rights: A status review. *Accounting, Auditing & Accountability Journal, 29*(4), 542–567. https://doi.org/10.1108/AAAJ-09-2015-2230

Meyer, J. W., & Rowan, B. (1977). Institutionalized organizations: Formal structure as myth and ceremony. *American Journal of Sociology, 83*(2), 340–363.

Mieszkowska, J. (2024). The unintended consequences of the EU corporate sustainability due diligence directive. *AJIL Unbound, 118*, 291–296. https://doi.org/10.1017/aju.2024.48

Monciardini, D., Bernaz, N., & Andhov, A. (2021). The organizational dynamics of compliance with the UK modern slavery act in the food and tobacco sector. *Business & Society, 60*(2), 288–340. https://doi.org/10.1177/0007650319898195

Montgomery, R. H., & Maggio, G. F. (2009). Fostering labor rights in developing countries: An investors' approach to managing labor issues. *Journal of Business Ethics, 87*(1), 199–219. https://doi.org/10.1007/s10551-008-9808-y

Morán-Muñoz, A., Fernández-Gago, R., & Godos-Díez, J. L. (2024). The impact of board gender and nationality diversity on corporate human rights performance in different institutional contexts. *Corporate Governance: An International Review*, 1–22. https://doi.org/10.1111/corg.12624

Moussa, T., Allam, A., & Elmarzouky, M. (2023). An examination of UK companies' modern slavery disclosure practices: Does board gender diversity matter? *Business Strategy and the Environment, 32*(8), 5382–5402. https://doi.org/10.1002/bse.3426

Muchlinski, P. (2012). Implementing the new UN corporate human rights framework: Implications for corporate law, governance, and regulation. *Business Ethics Quarterly, 22*(1), 145–177. https://doi.org/10.5840/beq20122218

Mukhtar, B., Shad, M. K., Ali, K., Woon, L. F., & Waqas, A. (2025). Systematic literature review and retrospective bibliometric analysis on ESG research. *International Journal of Productivity and Performance Management, 74*(4), 1365–1399. https://doi.org/10.1108/IJPPM-07-2023-0395

Muswaka, L. (2014). The corporate responsibility for human rights: A conceptual framework. *Mediterranean Journal of Social Sciences, 5*(3), 219–225. https://doi.org/10.5901/mjss.2014.v5n3p219

Nagaivska, D., & Uvarova, O. (2024). Companies operating in conflict-affected environments without impacting the conflict: Between regular and Heightened Human Rights Due Diligence. *Business and Human Rights Journal*, 1–6. https://doi.org/10.1017/bhj.2024.14

Nampoothiri, V. M., Entrop, O., & Annamalai, T. R. (2024). Effect of mandatory sustainability performance disclosures on firm value: Evidence from listed European firms.

Corporate Social Responsibility and Environmental Management, 31(6), 5220–5235. https://doi.org/10.1002/csr.2860

Narula, R. (2019). Enforcing higher labor standards within developing country value chains: Consequences for MNEs and informal actors in a dual economy. *Journal of International Business Studies, 50*(9), 1622–1635. https://doi.org/10.1057/s41267-019-00265-1

Neglia, M. (2016). The UNGPs — Five years on. *Netherlands Quarterly of Human Rights, 34*(4), 289–317. https://doi.org/10.1177/016934411603400403

Neri-Castracane, G., Canapa, D., & Brander, T. (2024). The Swiss legislation on business and human rights: A reform needed towards harmonization with EU law. *European Business Organization Law Review, 25*(4), 809–841. https://doi.org/10.1007/s40804-024-00325-6

Nicolò, G., Santis, S., Incollingo, A., & Tartaglia Polcini, P. (2024). Value relevance research in accounting and reporting domains: A bibliometric analysis. *Accounting in Europe, 21*(2), 176–211. https://doi.org/10.1080/17449480.2023.2292654

Nicolò, G., Zampone, G., Sannino, G., & Polcini, P. T. (2025). Ready for change after the omnibus package? Early compliance with the European sustainability reporting standards and its key determinants in the new regulatory era. *Business Strategy and the Environment*, 1–19. https://doi.org/10.1002/bse.70054

Nieri, F., Giuliani, E., & Fiaschi, D. (2023). Which norms do CSR help to respect? In *Research handbook on international corporate social responsibility* (pp. 108–126). Edward Elgar Publishing.

Nolan, J. (2022). Chasing the next shiny thing: Can human rights due diligence effectively address labour exploitation in global fashion supply chains? *International Journal for Crime, Justice and Social Democracy, 11*(2), 1–14. https://doi.org/10.5204/ijcjsd.2398

Nolan, J., & Taylor, L. (2009). Corporate responsibility for economic, social and cultural rights: Rights in search of a remedy? *Journal of Business Ethics, 87*(2), 433–451. https://doi.org/10.1007/s10551-009-0295-6

O'Donovan, G. (2002). Environmental disclosures in the annual report: Extending the applicability and predictive power of legitimacy theory. *Accounting, Auditing & Accountability Journal, 15*(3), 344–371. https://doi.org/10.1108/09513570210435870

Office of the United Nations High Commissioner for Human Rights (OHCHR). (2012). *The corporate responsibility to respect human rights: An interpretive guide*. United Nations. https://www.ohchr.org/sites/default/files/Documents/Publications/HR.PUB.12.2_En.pdf

Oliveira, C. R. D., & Silveira, R. A. D. (2023). Business and human rights: A tense, mined and contested field. *Organizações & Sociedade, 30*(106), 410–427. https://doi.org/10.1590/1984-9230202330n0014n

Oliver, C. (1991). Strategic responses to institutional processes. *Academy of Management Review, 16*(1), 145–179. https://doi.org/10.5465/amr.1991.4279002

Olsen, T., Rehbein, K., Snelson-Powell, A., & Westermann-Behaylo, M. (2022). Human rights in the oil and gas industry: When are policies and practices enough to prevent abuse? *Business and Society, 61*(6), 1512–1557. https://doi.org/10.1177/00076503211017435

Olsen, T. D., Schrempf-Stirling, J., & Van Buren, H. J. (2025). Classifying business and human rights thought in management scholarship. In *A research agenda for business and human rights* (pp. 1–18). Edward Elgar. https://doi.org/10.4337/9781802208979.00008

Page, M. J., McKenzie, J. E., Bossuyt, P. M., Boutron, I., Hoffmann, T. C., Mulrow, C. D., Shamseer, L., Tetzlaff, J. M., Akl, E. A., Brennan, S. E., Chou, R., Glanville, J., Grimshaw, J. M., Hróbjartsson, A., Lalu, M. M., Li, T., Loder, E. W., Mayo-Wilson, E., McDonald, S., et al. (2021). The PRISMA 2020 statement: An updated guideline for reporting systematic reviews. *BMJ, 372*, n71. https://doi.org/10.1136/bmj.n71

Palea, V., Santhià, C., & Miazza, A. (2023). Are circular economy strategies economically successful? Evidence from a longitudinal panel. *Journal of Environmental Management, 337*, 1–12. https://doi.org/10.1016/j.jenvman.2023.117726

Parella, K. (2019). Improving human rights compliance in supply chains. *Notre Dame Law Review, 95*(2), 727–793. https://scholarship.law.nd.edu/ndlr/vol95/iss2/5.

Patten, D. M. (2002). The relation between environmental performance and environmental disclosure: A research note. *Accounting, Organizations and Society, 27*(8), 763–773. https://doi.org/10.1016/S0361-3682(02)00028-4

Patterson, D. (2024). Human rights-based approaches and the right to health: A systematic literature review. *Journal of Human Rights Practice, 16*(2), 603–623. https://doi.org/10.1093/jhuman/huad063

Podrecca, M., Sartor, M., & Nassimbeni, G. (2022). United Nations Global Compact: Where are we going? *Social Responsibility Journal, 18*(5), 984–1003. https://doi.org/10.1108/SRJ-06-2020-0261

Preuss, L., & Brown, D. (2012). Business policies on human rights: An analysis of their content and prevalence among FTSE 100 firms. *Journal of Business Ethics, 109*(3), 289–299. https://doi.org/10.1007/s10551-011-1127-z

Principale, S. (2023). Human rights due diligence and corporate governance: A European analysis. In S. Marasca, A. M. Fellegara, & R. Mussari (Eds.), *Fostering sustainability in corporate governance, analysis of the EU sustainable corporate governance and due diligence directives* (pp. 63–76). Springer. https://doi.org/10.1007/978-3-031-30354-8

Quijano, G., & Lopez, C. (2021). Rise of mandatory human rights due diligence: A beacon of hope or a double-edged sword? *Business and Human Rights Journal, 6*(2), 241–254. https://doi.org/10.1017/bhj.2021.7

Ramasastry, A. (2015). Corporate social responsibility versus business and human rights: Bridging the gap between responsibility and accountability. *Journal of Human Rights, 14*(2), 237–259. https://doi.org/10.1080/14754835.2015.1037953

Rao, M., Bernaz, N., & de Boer, A. (2024). Holding retail corporations accountable for food waste: A due diligence framework informed by business and human rights principles. *Journal of Business Ethics, 193*(3), 679–689. https://doi.org/10.1007/s10551-023-05572-0

Rasche, A., & Waddock, S. (2021). The UN guiding principles on business and human rights: Implications for corporate social responsibility research. *Business and Human Rights Journal, 6*(2), 227–240. https://doi.org/10.1017/bhj.2021.2

Reiner, V., Malik, A., & Murray, J. (2025). Can global modern slavery be footprinted for corporate due diligence? A data review and analysis. *Journal of Industrial Ecology, 29*(4), 1077–1089. https://doi.org/10.1111/jiec.70037

Reinsberg, B., & Steinert, C. V. (2025). The French duty of vigilance law: Reconciling human rights and firm profitability. *Review of International Political Economy*, 1–33. https://doi.org/10.1080/09692290.2025.2519189

Rice, D. (2002). Human rights strategies for corporations. *Business Ethics: A European Review, 11*(2), 134–136. https://doi.org/10.1111/1467-8608.00268

Rogerson, M. (2024). Business and human rights in Russia: Emerging or merging? *Business and Human Rights Journal, 9*(1), 103–128. https://doi.org/10.1017/bhj.2022.29

Rogerson, M., Scarpa, F., & Snelson-Powell, A. (2024). Accounting for human rights: Evidence of due diligence in EU-listed firms' reporting. *Critical Perspectives on Accounting, 99*, 1–19. https://doi.org/10.1016/j.cpa.2024.102716

Romito, S., Vurro, C., & Aiello, B. (2025). The effectiveness of corporate human rights policies in preventing misbehavior: An empirical investigation in the garment industry. *EURAM Conference Proceedings*, 1–41.

Roszkowska-Menkes, M., Aluchna, M., & Kamiński, B. (2024). True transparency or mere decoupling? The study of selective disclosure in sustainability reporting. *Critical Perspectives on Accounting, 98*, 1–24. https://doi.org/10.1016/j.cpa.2023.102700

Ruggie, J. G. (2007). Business and human rights: The evolving international agenda. *American Journal of International Law, 101*(4), 819–840. https://doi.org/10.1017/S0002930000037738

Ruggie, J. (2013). *Just business: Multinational corporations and human rights*. W. W. Norton.

Salcito, K., & Wielga, M. (2018). What does human rights due diligence for business relationships really look like on the ground? *Business and Human Rights Journal, 3*(1), 113–121. https://doi.org/10.1017/bhj.2017.31

Sarfaty, G. A. (2021). Global supply chain auditing. In *The Cambridge handbook of compliance* (pp. 977–988). Cambridge University Press. https://doi.org/10.1017/9781108759458.067

Savage, A., Gilbert, E., Rowlands, J., & Cataldo, A. J. (2001). Environmental disclosure in annual reports: A legitimacy theory perspective. *South African Journal of Accounting Research, 15*(1), 19–48. https://doi.org/10.1080/10291954.2001.11435096

Schiller, F., & Prpich, G. (2014). Learning to organise risk management in organisations: What future for enterprise risk management? *Journal of Risk Research, 17*(8), 999–1017. https://doi.org/10.1080/13669877.2013.841725

Schilling-Vacaflor, A., & Lenschow, A. (2023). Hardening foreign corporate accountability through mandatory due diligence in the European Union? New trends and persisting challenges. *Regulation & Governance, 17*(3), 677–693. https://doi.org/10.1111/rego.12402

Schleper, M. C., Blome, C., Stevenson, M., Thürer, M., & Tusell, I. (2022). When it's the slaves that pay: In search of a fair due diligence cost distribution in conflict mineral supply chains. *Transportation Research Part E: Logistics and Transportation Review, 164*, 1–17. https://doi.org/10.1016/j.tre.2022.102801

Schrempf-Stirling, J., & Van Buren, H. J. (2020). Business and human rights scholarship in social issues in management: An analytical review. *Business and Human Rights Journal, 5*(1), 28–55. https://doi.org/10.1017/bhj.2019.23

Schrempf-Stirling, J., & Van Buren, H. J. (2024). The importance of human rights for management and organization studies. *British Journal of Management, 35*, 1127–1140. https://doi.org/10.1111/1467-8551.12799

Schrempf-Stirling, J., Van Buren, H. J., & Wettstein, F. (2022). Human rights: A promising perspective for business & society. *Business & Society, 61*(5), 1282–1321. https://doi.org/10.1177/00076503211068425

Shavin, C. (2019). Unlocking the potential of the new OECD due diligence guidance on responsible business conduct. *Business and Human Rights Journal, 4*(1), 139–145. https://doi.org/10.1017/bhj.2018.28

Sherman, J. F. (2022). *Human rights due diligence and corporate governance*. SSRN, 1–35. https://doi.org/10.2139/ssrn.4066743

Shift. (2017). *An open letter to United Nations Secretary-General António Guterres and United Nations Private Sector Forum 2017 participants*. https://shiftproject.org/open-letter-on-human-rights-and-the-sustainable-development-goals/

Shulman, S. (2024). Corporate sustainability due diligence: Combining human rights and the environment. *Columbia Journal of Environmental Law, 49*(2), 479–523.

Slawotsky, J. (2023). Leveraging human rights due diligence in corporate-state procurement: The exemplar of the Pfizer-Israeli COVID-19 vaccination program. *Business and Human Rights Journal, 8*(3), 352–368. https://doi.org/10.1017/bhj.2023.43

Smit, L., Bright, C., Pietropaoli, I., Hughes-Jennett, J., & Hood, P. (2020). Business views on mandatory human rights due diligence regulation: A comparative analysis of two recent studies. *Business and Human Rights Journal, 5*(2), 261–269. https://doi.org/10.1017/bhj.2020.10

Smith, E. K., Kolcava, D., & Bernauer, T. (2024). Stringent sustainability regulations for global supply chains are supported across middle-income democracies. *Nature Communications, 15*(1), 1–12. https://doi.org/10.1038/s41467-024-45399-5

Stein, M. A., & Bantekas, I. (2021). Including disability in business and human rights discourse and corporate practice. *Business and Human Rights Journal, 6*(3), 490–513. https://doi.org/10.1017/bhj.2021.13

Suchman, M. C. (1995). Managing legitimacy: Strategic and institutional approaches. *The Academy of Management Review, 20*(3), 571–610. https://doi.org/10.2307/258788

Szablewska, N., & Kubacki, K. (2023). Empirical business research on modern slavery in supply chains: A systematic review. *Journal of Business Research, 164*. https://doi.org/10.1016/j.jbusres.2023.113988

Thorens, M., Bernaz, N., & Hospes, O. (2025). Advocating for the EU corporate sustainability due diligence directive against the odds: Strategies and legitimation. *Journal of Common Market Studies, 63*(2), 606–623. https://doi.org/10.1111/jcms.13623

Torelli, R., Fiandrino, S., & Scarpa, F. (2024). Value-enhancing drivers of corporate governance in improving human rights due diligence: Worldwide evidence. *Corporate Social Responsibility and Environmental Management*, 1–12. https://doi.org/10.1002/csr.3001

Triefus, S. (2023). The UNGPs and ISDS: Should businesses assess the human rights impacts of investor-state arbitration? *Business and Human Rights Journal, 8*(3), 329–351. https://doi.org/10.1017/bhj.2023.45

Tsalis, T. A., Terzaki, M., Koulouriotis, D., Tsagarakis, K. P., & Nikolaou, I. E. (2023). The nexus of United Nations' 2030 Agenda and corporate sustainability reports. *Sustainable Development, 31*(2), 784–796. https://doi.org/10.1002/sd.2419

Ullah, S., Adams, K., Adams, D., & Attah-Boakye, R. (2021). Multinational corporations and human rights violations in emerging economies: Does commitment to social and environmental responsibility matter? *Journal of Environmental Management, 280*, 1–13. https://doi.org/10.1016/j.jenvman.2020.111689

United Nations Global Compact (UNGC). (2020). *Principles*. https://www.unglobalcompact.org/what-is-gc/mission/principles

United Nations Human Rights Council (UNHRC). (2011). *Guiding principles on business and human rights: Implementing the United Nations "Protect, Respect and Remedy" framework* (A/HRC/17/31). https://www.ohchr.org/documents/publications/guidingprinciplesbusinesshr_en.pdf

Van Buren, H. J., Schrempf-Stirling, J., & Westermann-Behaylo, M. (2021). Business and human trafficking: A social connection and political responsibility model. *Business and Society, 60*(2), 341–375. https://doi.org/10.1177/0007650319872509

van der Ploeg, L., & Vanclay, F. (2017). A tool for improving the management of social and human rights risks at project sites: The Human Rights Sphere. *Journal of Cleaner Production, 142*, 4072–4084. https://doi.org/10.1016/j.jclepro.2016.10.028

Voss, H. (2020). Implications of the COVID-19 pandemic for human rights and modern slavery vulnerabilities in global value chains. *Transnational Corporations, 27*(2), 113–125.

Wahab, A. A. B. (2020). Human rights anchored in business: Practice and challenges in the palm oil sector in Malaysia. *International Studies Review, 20*(1), 1–20. https://doi.org/10.1163/2667078-02001006

Wang, S. L., Lee, Y., & Li, D. (2024). Smart disclosure: An enabler for multinationals to reduce human rights violations in global supply chains. *Journal of International Business Studies, 55*(4), 450–469. https://doi.org/10.1057/s41267-024-00698-3

Webster, J., & Watson, R. T. (2002). Analyzing the past to prepare for the future: Writing a literature review. *MIS Quarterly, 26*(2), 8–23. https://doi.org/10.2307/4132319

Welford, R. (2002). Globalization, corporate social responsibility and human rights. *Corporate Social Responsibility and Environmental Management, 9*, 1–7. https://doi.org/10.1002/csr.4

Wettstein, F. (2010). The duty to protect: Corporate complicity, political responsibility, and human rights advocacy. *Journal of Business Ethics, 96*(1), 33–47. https://doi.org/10.1007/s10551-010-0447-8

Wettstein, F. (2012). CSR and the debate on business and human rights: Bridging the great divide. *Business Ethics Quarterly, 22*(4), 739–770. https://doi.org/10.5840/beq201222446

Wettstein, F. (2013). Making noise about silent complicity: The moral inconsistency of the 'Protect, Respect and Remedy' framework. In *Human rights obligations of business: Beyond the corporate responsibility to respect?* (pp. 243–268). Cambridge University Press. https://doi.org/10.1017/CBO9781139568333.015

Wettstein, F. (2020). The history of business and human rights and its relationship with corporate social responsibility. In *Research handbook on human rights and business*. Elgar. https://doi.org/10.4337/9781786436405.00007

Wettstein, F. (2021). Betting on the wrong (Trojan) horse: CSR and the implementation of the UN Guiding Principles on Business and Human Rights. *Business and Human Rights Journal, 6*(2), 312–325. https://doi.org/10.1017/bhj.2021.21

Wettstein, F. (2022). *Business and human rights: Overcoming old paradigms, pushing for new frontiers written by Florian Wettstein business and human rights: Overcoming old paradigms, pushing for new frontiers*. https://www.e-ir.info/2022/01/09/business-and-human-rights-overcoming-old-paradigms-pushing-for-new-frontiers/

Wettstein, F. (2025). Back to the future: From 'business and human rights' to a rightsholder-centered economy. In T. Olsen, J. Schrempf-Stirling, & H. J. Van Buren III (Eds.), *A research agenda for business and human rights* (pp. 205–210). ElgarOnline.

Wettstein, F., Giuliani, E., Santangelo, G. D., & Stahl, G. K. (2019). International business and human rights: A research agenda. *Journal of World Business, 54*(1), 54–65. https://doi.org/10.1016/j.jwb.2018.10.004

Wilhelm, M. (2024). Mandatory due diligence legislation: A paradigm shift for the governance of sustainability in global value chains? *Journal of International Business Policy, 7*(4), 459–465. https://doi.org/10.1057/s42214-024-00193-4

Winkler, I. T., & Williams, C. (2017). The Sustainable Development Goals and human rights: A critical early review. *The International Journal of Human Rights, 21*(8), 1023–1028. https://doi.org/10.1080/13642987.2017.1348695

Wörsdörfer, M. (2015). The equator principles and human rights due diligence – Towards a positive and leverage-based concept of corporate social responsibility. *Philosophy of Management, 14*(3), 193–218. https://doi.org/10.1007/s40926-015-0014-6

Zagelmeyer, S. (2020). MNEs and human rights: From responsibilities to rights to governance. *Critical Perspectives on International Business, 16*(2), 117–135. https://doi.org/10.1108/cpoib-07-2018-0063

Zagelmeyer, S., & Sinkovics, R. R. (2019). MNEs, human rights and the SDGs – The moderating role of business and human rights governance. *Transnational Corporations Journal, 26*(3), 33–62. https://unctad.org/en/PublicationChapters/diaeia20193a2_en.pdf

Zampella, A., Campanella, F., Serino, L., & Spignese, A. (2025). Do effective and sustainable corporate governance mechanisms affect the relevance of non-financial information? *Corporate Social Responsibility and Environmental Management, 32*(1), 741–756. https://doi.org/10.1002/csr.2989

Kolibri 360 GmbH
Ferdinand-Jühlke-Straße 7
99095 Erfurt, Deutschland
produktsicherheit@kolibri360.de